ISBN 0-8373-0665-5

C-665   CAREER EXAMINATION SERIES

This is your
PASSBOOK® for...

Ranger, U.S. Park Service

Test Preparation Study Guide

Questions & Answers

NATIONAL LEARNING CORPORATION

PASSBOOK®

NOTICE

PASSBOOK SERIES®

THE *PASSBOOK SERIES®* has been created to prepare applicants and candidates for the ultimate academic battlefield – the examination room.

At some time in our lives, each and every one of us may be required to take an examination – for validation, matriculation, admission, qualification, registration, certification, or licensure.

Based on the assumption that every applicant or candidate has met the basic formal educational standards, has taken the required number of courses, and read the necessary texts, the *PASSBOOK SERIES®* furnishes the one special preparation which may assure passing with confidence, instead of failing with insecurity. Examination questions – together with answers – are furnished as the basic vehicle for study so that the mysteries of the examination and its compounding difficulties may be eliminated or diminished by a sure method.

This book is meant to help you pass your examination provided that you qualify and are serious in your objective.

The entire field is reviewed through the huge store of content information which is succinctly presented through a provocative and challenging approach – the question-and-answer method.

A climate of success is established by furnishing the correct answers at the end of each test.

You soon learn to recognize types of questions, forms of questions, and patterns of questioning. You may even begin to anticipate expected outcomes.

You perceive that many questions are repeated or adapted so that you can gain acute insights, which may enable you to score many sure points.

You learn how to confront new questions, or types of questions, and to attack them confidently and work out the correct answers.

You note objectives and emphases, and recognize pitfalls and dangers, so that you may make positive educational adjustments.

Moreover, you are kept fully informed in relation to new concepts, methods, practices, and directions in the field.

You discover that you are actually taking the examination all the time: you are preparing for the examination by "taking" an examination, not by reading extraneous and/or supererogatory textbooks.

In short, this PASSBOOK®, used directedly, should be an important factor in helping you to pass your test.

CONSERVATION OCCUPATIONS

CONSERVATION OCCUPATIONS

Forests, rangelands, wildlife, and water are part of our country's great wealth of natural resources. Conservationists project, develop, and manage natural resources to assure that they are not needlessly exhausted, destroyed, or damaged, and that future needs for the resources will be met.

Specialized training is generally required to work in conservation occupations. Many positions can be filled only by those having a bachelor's degree. For other positions, the desired training may be obtained on the job.

This section includes descriptions of three conservation occupations -- forester, forestry aid, and range manager. Other conservation workers include soil conservationists.

FORESTERS

NATURE OF WORK

Forests are one of America's greatest natural resources, covering more than one-third of the land area of the country. Foresters manage, develop, and protect these valuable lands and their resources--timber, water, wildlife, forage, and recreation areas. They estimate the amount and value of these resources. They plan and supervise the harvesting and cutting of trees, purchase and sale of trees and timber, and reforestation activities (renewing the forest cover by seeding or planting). Foresters also safeguard forests from fire, destructive animals and insects, and diseases. Some foresters are responsible for wildlife protection and watershed management, as well as for the management of camps, parks, and grazing land.

Foresters usually specialize in one area of work such as timber management, fire control, forest economics, outdoor recreation, watershed management, wildlife management, or range management. Some of these areas are becoming recognized as distinct professions. The profession of range managers, for example, is discussed in a separate statement in this section. Foresters may also specialize in such activities as research, writing and editing, extension work (providing forestry information to farmers, logging companies, and the public), forest marketing, and college and university teaching.

TRAINING, OTHER QUALIFICATIONS, AND ADVANCEMENT

A bachelor's degree with a major in forestry is the usual minimum educational requirement for young persons seeking professional careers in forestry. An advanced degree is generally required for teaching and research positions.

Training in forestry leading to a bachelor's or higher degree was offered in colleges and universities. The curriculums in most of these schools include specialized forestry courses in five essential areas: (1) silviculture (methods of growing and improving forest crops); (2) forest protection (primarily against fire, insects, and disease); (3) forest management (the application of business methods and technical forestry principles to the operation of a forest property); (4) forest economics (study of the factors affecting the supply of and the demand for forest products) and (5) forest utilization (the harvesting, processing, and marketing of the forest crop and other forest resources). The curriculums also include related courses in the management of recreational lands, watershed management, and wildlife management, as well as courses in mathematics, science, engineering, economics, and the humanities. In addition, the great majority of colleges require that students spend one summer in a field camp operated by the college. Forestry students are also encouraged to work other summers in jobs that will give them firsthand experience in forest or conservation work.

Beginning positions for forestry graduates often involve performing routine duties under the supervision of experienced foresters. As they gain experience and are given more responsibility, foresters may advance to positions such as that of branch forester, district ranger, forest supervisor, and managing forester.

Qualifications for success in forestry include an enthusiasm for outdoor work and the ability to meet and deal effectively with people. Many jobs also require physical stamina and a willingness to work in remote areas.

EMPLOYMENT OUTLOOK

Employment opportunities for forestry graduates are expected to be favorable through the 1990's. There will be a strong demand for well-qualified personnel with advanced degrees for college teaching positions and for research in areas such as forest genetics, forest diseases and insects, forest products utilization, and fire behavior and control. Among the major factors underlying this anticipated demand are the country's growing population and rising living standards, which will tend to increase the demand for forest products, and the use of forests for recreation areas.

2

Private owners of timberland are expected to offer increasing numbers of employment opportunities to foresters, because they are becoming increasingly aware of the profitability of improved forestry and logging practices. The forest products industries also will require additional foresters to apply new techniques for utilizing the entire forest crop, and for cutting trees once regarded as unprofitable for timber operations. In addition, competition from metal, plastics, and other materials is expected to stimulate further research to develop new and improved wood products.

The Federal Government is likely to offer increasing employment opportunities for foresters in the years ahead, mainly in the Forest Service of the Department of Agriculture. Among the factors expected to contribute to this expansion are the demands for the use of national forest resources, the trend toward more scientific management of these lands, and expanding research programs in areas such as outdoor recreation, watershed management, wildlife protection, and range management.

State government agencies should also offer additional employment opportunities for foresters. Forest fire control, protection against insects and diseases, provision of technical assistance to owners of private forest lands, and other Federal-State co-operative programs are usually channeled through State forestry organizations. Growing demands for recreation facilities in forest lands are likely to result in expansion of State parks and other recreational areas.

In addition to new positions created by the rising demand for foresters, a few hundred openings will arise each year owing to retirements, deaths, and transfers out of the profession.

Opportunities for women in outdoor forestry work will probably continue to be limited, largely because of the strenuous physical requirements of much of the work. The few women presently employed in forestry are engaged chiefly in research, administration, and educational work, and future opportunities for women are also likely to be primarily in these fields.

FORESTRY AIDS

NATURE OF WORK

Forestry aids, sometimes called forestry technicians, assist foresters in managing and caring for both public and private forest lands. Some of their duties include estimating the amount, growth, and value of timber in a forest by sampling techniques; marking timber for harvest; pruning trees to improve the quality of the timber; spraying trees with pesticides to protect them from insects and diseases; collecting information on the condition of watershed projects; and investigating the causes of stream and lake pollution. Forestry aids also conduct road surveys and maintain forest trails. They may supervise timber sale operations and manage recreation facilities.

Forestry aids may be engaged in all phases of fire prevention and control. If a fire occurs, they may lead fire fighting crews. After the fire has been suppressed, they take inventory of the burned out area and plant new trees and shrubs. Fire precautions are also stressed by the aids as they instruct persons using the forest for recreation purposes to assure that no harm will come to them or to the forest.

Some aids employed in laboratories assist scientists in tests and experiments to discover ways to expand the utilization of forest products.

WHERE EMPLOYED

Forestry aids are located chiefly in the heavily forested States of Washington, California, Oregon, Idaho, Utah, and Montana.

TRAINING, OTHER QUALIFICATIONS, AND ADVANCEMENT

Young persons qualify for beginning positions as forestry aids either by completing a specialized 1-or 2-year post-secondary school curriculum or through work experience. Curriculums designed to train forestry aids are offered in technical institutes, junior colleges, and ranger schools (schools that specialize in training forestry aids). Among the specialized courses are forest mensuration (measurement of the number and size of trees in the forest), forest protection, dendrology (identification of trees and shrubs), wood utilization, and silviculture (methods of growing and improving forest crops). In addition, the student takes courses, such as drafting, surveying, report writing, and first aid and spends time in a forest or camp operated by the school, where he obtains experience in forestry work.

Persons who have not had post-secondary school training must usually have had experience in forest work, such as felling or planting trees and fighting fires, to qualify for beginning forestry aid jobs. In the Federal Government, the minimum experience requirement is two seasons of related work. Those who have had some technical experience such as estimating timber resources may qualify for more responsible positions.

Qualifications considered essential for success in this field are an enthusiasm for outdoor work, physical stamina, and the ability to carry out tasks without direct supervision. Many jobs also require a willingness to work in remote areas.

EMPLOYMENT OUTLOOK

Employment opportunities for forestry aids are expected to be good through the 1990's. Prospects will be especially good for those with post-high school training in a forestry curriculum. As the employment of foresters continues to grow, increasing numbers of forestry aids will be needed to assist them. Also, it is expected that forestry aids will assume some of the more routine jobs being done by foresters.

Private industry is expected to provide many additional employment opportunities for forestry aids. Forest products industries are becoming increasingly aware of the profitability of employing technical persons knowledgeable in the practical application of scientific forest practices.

The Federal Government is also likely to offer increasing employment opportunities for forestry aids through the 1990's, mainly in the Forest Service of the Department of Agriculture. Similarly, State governments will probably increase their employment of forestry aids. Growth in Government employment will stem from factors such as increasing demand for recreational facilities, the trend toward more scientific management of forest land and water supplies, and an increasing amount of timber cutting on Federal forest land.

RANGE MANAGERS

NATURE OF WORK

Rangelands cover more than 700 million acres in the United States, mostly in the Western and Southern States. Range managers, also called range conservationists or range scientists, are responsible for the management, development, and protection of these rangelands and their resources. They establish systems and plans for grazing that will yield the highest production of livestock while preserving conditions of soil and vegetation necessary to meet other land-use requirements -- wildlife grazing, recreation, growing timber, and watersheds. Range managers evaluate forage resources; estimate the amount of forage that can be properly utilized; decide on the number and appropriate type of livestock to be grazed and the best season for grazing; restore deteriorated rangelands through seeding or plant control; and determine other range conservation and development needs. Range fire protection, pest control, and grazing trespass control are also important areas of work.

The range managers' activities may include research in range maintenance and improvement, report writing, teaching, extension work (providing information about range management to holders of privately owned grazing lands), or performing technical assignments in foreign countries.

TRAINING, OTHER QUALIFICATIONS, AND ADVANCEMENT

The bachelor's degree with a major in range management or range conservation is the usual requirement for persons seeking employment as range managers in the Federal Government. A bachelor's degree in a closely related subject-matter field, such as agronomy, animal husbandry, botany, forestry, soil conservation, or wildlife management, with courses in range management and range conservation, is also accepted as adequate preparation. Graduate degrees are generally required for teaching and research work.

Training leading to a bachelor's degree with a major in range management was offered by colleges and universities, mainly in Western and Southwestern States. Most schools conferring the bachelor's degree in range management also grant the master's degree, and a few such schools award the doctorate.

The essential courses for a degree in range management are botany, plant ecology, and plant physiology; zoology; animal husbandry; soils; chemistry; mathematics; and special courses in range management, such as identification and characteristics of range plants, range management principles and practices, and range management methods and techniques. Desirable elective courses include economics, statistical methods, physics, geology, watershed management, wildlife management, surveying, and forage crops.

Federal Government agencies -- primarily the Forest Service and the Bureau of Land Management -- hire many college juniors and seniors for summer jobs in range management. This experience helps students qualify for permanent positions as range managers when they complete college.

Because most range managers must meet and deal with other people, individually or in groups, they should be able to communicate their ideas effectively, both in writing and speaking. Many jobs require the stamina to perform vigorous physical activity, and a willingness to work in arid and sparsely populated areas.

EMPLOYMENT OUTLOOK

Employment opportunities for graduates with degrees in range management are expected to be favorable through the 1990's. The demand will be especially good for well-qualified persons with advanced degrees to fill research and teaching positions.

Opportunities will probably be best in Federal agencies. Favorable opportunities are also expected in private industry, since range livestock producers and private timber operators are hiring increasing numbers of range managers to improve their range holdings. Some openings are expected for range managers to give technical assistance overseas, particularly in developing countries of the Middle East, Africa, and South America.

Among the major factors underlying the anticipated growth in demand for range managers are population growth, increasing per capita consumption of animal products, and the growing use of rangelands for hunting and other recreational pursuits. Many openings are expected because of the more intensive management of range resources with increasing emphasis on multiple uses of rangelands. Range managers will also be needed to help rehabilitate deteriorated rangelands, improve semiarid lands, and deal with watershed problems. Along with growing demand for range managers, an increase is expected in the number of range management graduates. In the past, however, the annual number of graduates with degrees in range management was small. For example, according to the Range Management Education Council, in one year only 157 bachelor's degrees, 34 master's degrees, and 8 Ph.D. degrees were granted in this field. Therefore, unless the number of graduates should increase substantially, college graduates with degrees in range management should have favorable employment opportunities.

Opportunities for women in this profession are limited because of the rigorous work generally required, and the remote locations of employment. However, a few women, usually with training in botany, work on classification and identification of range plants.

HOW TO TAKE A TEST

I. YOU MUST PASS AN EXAMINATION

A. WHAT EVERY CANDIDATE SHOULD KNOW

Examination applicants often ask us for help in preparing for the written test. What can I study in advance? What kinds of questions will be asked? How will the test be given? How will the papers be graded?

As an applicant for a civil service examination, you may be wondering about some of these things. Our purpose here is to suggest effective methods of advance study and to describe civil service examinations.

Your chances for success on this examination can be increased if you know how to prepare. Those "pre-examination jitters" can be reduced if you know what to expect. You can even experience an adventure in good citizenship if you know why civil service exams are given.

B. WHY ARE CIVIL SERVICE EXAMINATIONS GIVEN?

Civil service examinations are important to you in two ways. As a citizen, you want public jobs filled by employees who know how to do their work. As a job seeker, you want a fair chance to compete for that job on an equal footing with other candidates. The best-known means of accomplishing this two-fold goal is the competitive examination.

Exams are widely publicized throughout the nation. They may be administered for jobs in federal, state, city, municipal, town or village governments or agencies.

Any citizen may apply, with some limitations, such as the age or residence of applicants. Your experience and education may be reviewed to see whether you meet the requirements for the particular examination. When these requirements exist, they are reasonable and applied consistently to all applicants. Thus, a competitive examination may cause you some uneasiness now, but it is your privilege and safeguard.

C. HOW ARE CIVIL SERVICE EXAMS DEVELOPED?

Examinations are carefully written by trained technicians who are specialists in the field known as "psychological measurement," in consultation with recognized authorities in the field of work that the test will cover. These experts recommend the subject matter areas or skills to be tested; only those knowledges or skills important to your success on the job are included. The most reliable books and source materials available are used as references. Together, the experts and technicians judge the difficulty level of the questions.

Test technicians know how to phrase questions so that the problem is clearly stated. Their ethics do not permit "trick" or "catch" questions. Questions may have been tried out on sample groups, or subjected to statistical analysis, to determine their usefulness.

Written tests are often used in combination with performance tests, ratings of training and experience, and oral interviews. All of these measures combine to form the best-known means of finding the right person for the right job.

II. HOW TO PASS THE WRITTEN TEST

A. NATURE OF THE EXAMINATION

To prepare intelligently for civil service examinations, you should know how they differ from school examinations you have taken. In school you were assigned certain definite pages to read or subjects to cover. The examination questions were quite detailed and usually emphasized memory. Civil service exams, on the other hand, try to discover your present ability to perform the duties of a position, plus your potentiality to learn these duties. In other words, a civil service exam attempts to predict how successful you will be. Questions cover such a broad area that they cannot be as minute and detailed as school exam questions.

In the public service similar kinds of work, or positions, are grouped together in one "class." This process is known as *position-classification*. All the positions in a class are paid according to the salary range for that class. One class title covers all of these positions, and they are all tested by the same examination.

B. FOUR BASIC STEPS

1) Study the announcement

How, then, can you know what subjects to study? Our best answer is: "Learn as much as possible about the class of positions for which you've applied." The exam will test the knowledge, skills and abilities needed to do the work.

Your most valuable source of information about the position you want is the official exam announcement. This announcement lists the training and experience qualifications. Check these standards and apply only if you come reasonably close to meeting them.

The brief description of the position in the examination announcement offers some clues to the subjects which will be tested. Think about the job itself. Review the duties in your mind. Can you perform them, or are there some in which you are rusty? Fill in the blank spots in your preparation.

Many jurisdictions preview the written test in the exam announcement by including a section called "Knowledge and Abilities Required," "Scope of the Examination," or some similar heading. Here you will find out specifically what fields will be tested.

2) Review your own background

Once you learn in general what the position is all about, and what you need to know to do the work, ask yourself which subjects you already know fairly well and which need improvement. You may wonder whether to concentrate on improving your strong areas or on building some background in your fields of weakness. When the announcement has specified "some knowledge" or "considerable knowledge," or has used adjectives like "beginning principles of…" or "advanced … methods," you can get a clue as to the number and difficulty of questions to be asked in any given field. More questions, and hence broader coverage, would be included for those subjects which are more important in the work. Now weigh your strengths and weaknesses against the job requirements and prepare accordingly.

3) Determine the level of the position

Another way to tell how intensively you should prepare is to understand the level of the job for which you are applying. Is it the entering level? In other words, is this the position in which beginners in a field of work are hired? Or is it an intermediate or advanced level? Sometimes this is indicated by such words as "Junior" or "Senior" in the class title. Other jurisdictions use Roman numerals to designate the level – Clerk I, Clerk II, for example. The word "Supervisor" sometimes appears in the title. If the level is not indicated by the title, check the description of duties. Will you be working under very close supervision, or will you have responsibility for independent decisions in this work?

4) Choose appropriate study materials

Now that you know the subjects to be examined and the relative amount of each subject to be covered, you can choose suitable study materials. For beginning level jobs, or even advanced ones, if you have a pronounced weakness in some aspect of your training, read a modern, standard textbook in that field. Be sure it is up to date and has general coverage. Such books are normally available at your library, and the librarian will be glad to help you locate one. For entry-level positions, questions of appropriate difficulty are chosen – neither highly advanced questions, nor those too simple. Such questions require careful thought but not advanced training.

If the position for which you are applying is technical or advanced, you will read more advanced, specialized material. If you are already familiar with the basic principles of your field, elementary textbooks would waste your time. Concentrate on advanced textbooks and technical periodicals. Think through the concepts and review difficult problems in your field.

These are all general sources. You can get more ideas on your own initiative, following these leads. For example, training manuals and publications of the government agency which employs workers in your field can be useful, particularly for technical and professional positions. A letter or visit to the government department involved may result in more specific study suggestions, and certainly will provide you with a more definite idea of the exact nature of the position you are seeking.

III. KINDS OF TESTS

Tests are used for purposes other than measuring knowledge and ability to perform specified duties. For some positions, it is equally important to test ability to make adjustments to new situations or to profit from training. In others, basic mental abilities not dependent on information are essential. Questions which test these things may not appear as pertinent to the duties of the position as those which test for knowledge and information. Yet they are often highly important parts of a fair examination. For very general questions, it is almost impossible to help you direct your study efforts. What we can do is to point out some of the more common of these general abilities needed in public service positions and describe some typical questions.

1) General information

Broad, general information has been found useful for predicting job success in some kinds of work. This is tested in a variety of ways, from vocabulary lists to questions about current events. Basic background in some field of work, such as sociology or economics, may be sampled in a group of questions. Often these are principles which have become familiar to most persons through exposure rather than through formal training. It is difficult to advise you how to study for these questions; being alert to the world around you is our best suggestion.

2) Verbal ability

An example of an ability needed in many positions is verbal or language ability. Verbal ability is, in brief, the ability to use and understand words. Vocabulary and grammar tests are typical measures of this ability. Reading comprehension or paragraph interpretation questions are common in many kinds of civil service tests. You are given a paragraph of written material and asked to find its central meaning.

3) Numerical ability

Number skills can be tested by the familiar arithmetic problem, by checking paired lists of numbers to see which are alike and which are different, or by interpreting charts and graphs. In the latter test, a graph may be printed in the test booklet which you are asked to use as the basis for answering questions.

4) Observation

A popular test for law-enforcement positions is the observation test. A picture is shown to you for several minutes, then taken away. Questions about the picture test your ability to observe both details and larger elements.

5) Following directions

In many positions in the public service, the employee must be able to carry out written instructions dependably and accurately. You may be given a chart with several columns, each column listing a variety of information. The questions require you to carry out directions involving the information given in the chart.

6) Skills and aptitudes

Performance tests effectively measure some manual skills and aptitudes. When the skill is one in which you are trained, such as typing or shorthand, you can practice. These tests are often very much like those given in business school or high school courses. For many of the other skills and aptitudes, however, no short-time preparation can be made. Skills and abilities natural to you or that you have developed throughout your lifetime are being tested.

Many of the general questions just described provide all the data needed to answer the questions and ask you to use your reasoning ability to find the answers. Your best preparation for these tests, as well as for tests of facts and ideas, is to be at your physical and mental best. You, no doubt, have your own methods of getting into an exam-taking mood and keeping "in shape." The next section lists some ideas on this subject.

IV. KINDS OF QUESTIONS

Only rarely is the "essay" question, which you answer in narrative form, used in civil service tests. Civil service tests are usually of the short-answer type. Full instructions for answering these questions will be given to you at the examination. But in case this is your first experience with short-answer questions and separate answer sheets, here is what you need to know:

1) Multiple-choice Questions

Most popular of the short-answer questions is the "multiple choice" or "best answer" question. It can be used, for example, to test for factual knowledge, ability to solve problems or judgment in meeting situations found at work.

A multiple-choice question is normally one of three types—

- It can begin with an incomplete statement followed by several possible endings. You are to find the one ending which *best* completes the statement, although some of the others may not be entirely wrong.
- It can also be a complete statement in the form of a question which is answered by choosing one of the statements listed.
- It can be in the form of a problem – again you select the best answer.

Here is an example of a multiple-choice question with a discussion which should give you some clues as to the method for choosing the right answer:

When an employee has a complaint about his assignment, the action which will *best* help him overcome his difficulty is to
- A. discuss his difficulty with his coworkers
- B. take the problem to the head of the organization
- C. take the problem to the person who gave him the assignment
- D. say nothing to anyone about his complaint

In answering this question, you should study each of the choices to find which is best. Consider choice "A" – Certainly an employee may discuss his complaint with fellow employees, but no change or improvement can result, and the complaint remains unresolved. Choice "B" is a poor choice since the head of the organization probably does not know what assignment you have been given, and taking your problem to him is known as "going over the head" of the supervisor. The supervisor, or person who made the assignment, is the person who can clarify it or correct any injustice. Choice "C" is, therefore, correct. To say nothing, as in choice "D," is unwise. Supervisors have and interest in knowing the problems employees are facing, and the employee is seeking a solution to his problem.

2) True/False Questions

The "true/false" or "right/wrong" form of question is sometimes used. Here a complete statement is given. Your job is to decide whether the statement is right or wrong.

SAMPLE: A person-to-person long-distance telephone call costs less than a station-to-station call to the same city.

This statement is wrong, or false, since person-to-person calls are more expensive.

This is not a complete list of all possible question forms, although most of the others are variations of these common types. You will always get complete directions for answering questions. Be sure you understand *how* to mark your answers – ask questions until you do.

V. RECORDING YOUR ANSWERS

For an examination with very few applicants, you may be told to record your answers in the test booklet itself. Separate answer sheets are much more common. If this separate answer sheet is to be scored by machine – and this is often the case – it is highly important that you mark your answers correctly in order to get credit.

An electric scoring machine is often used in civil service offices because of the speed with which papers can be scored. Machine-scored answer sheets must be marked with a pencil, which will be given to you. This pencil has a high graphite content which responds to the electric scoring machine. As a matter of fact, stray dots may register as answers, so do not let your pencil rest on the answer sheet while you are pondering the correct answer. Also, if your pencil lead breaks or is otherwise defective, ask for another.

Since the answer sheet will be dropped in a slot in the scoring machine, be careful not to bend the corners or get the paper crumpled.

The answer sheet normally has five vertical columns of numbers, with 30 numbers to a column. These numbers correspond to the question numbers in your test booklet. After each number, going across the page are four or five pairs of dotted lines. These short dotted lines have small letters or numbers above them. The first two pairs may also have a "T" or "F" above the letters. This indicates that the first two pairs only are to be used if the questions are of the true-false type. If the questions are multiple choice, disregard the "T" and "F" and pay attention only to the small letters or numbers.

Answer your questions in the manner of the sample that follows:

32. The largest city in the United States is
A. Washington, D.C.
B. New York City
C. Chicago
D. Detroit
E. San Francisco

1) Choose the answer you think is best. (New York City is the largest, so "B" is correct.)
2) Find the row of dotted lines numbered the same as the question you are answering. (Find row number 32)
3) Find the pair of dotted lines corresponding to the answer. (Find the pair of lines under the mark "B.")
4) Make a solid black mark between the dotted lines.

VI. BEFORE THE TEST

Common sense will help you find procedures to follow to get ready for an examination. Too many of us, however, overlook these sensible measures. Indeed, nervousness and fatigue have been found to be the most serious reasons why applicants fail to do their best on civil service tests. Here is a list of reminders:

- Begin your preparation early – Don't wait until the last minute to go scurrying around for books and materials or to find out what the position is all about.
- Prepare continuously – An hour a night for a week is better than an all-night cram session. This has been definitely established. What is more, a night a

week for a month will return better dividends than crowding your study into a shorter period of time.

- Locate the place of the exam – You have been sent a notice telling you when and where to report for the examination. If the location is in a different town or otherwise unfamiliar to you, it would be well to inquire the best route and learn something about the building.
- Relax the night before the test – Allow your mind to rest. Do not study at all that night. Plan some mild recreation or diversion; then go to bed early and get a good night's sleep.
- Get up early enough to make a leisurely trip to the place for the test – This way unforeseen events, traffic snarls, unfamiliar buildings, etc. will not upset you.
- Dress comfortably – A written test is not a fashion show. You will be known by number and not by name, so wear something comfortable.
- Leave excess paraphernalia at home – Shopping bags and odd bundles will get in your way. You need bring only the items mentioned in the official notice you received; usually everything you need is provided. Do not bring reference books to the exam. They will only confuse those last minutes and be taken away from you when in the test room.
- Arrive somewhat ahead of time – If because of transportation schedules you must get there very early, bring a newspaper or magazine to take your mind off yourself while waiting.
- Locate the examination room – When you have found the proper room, you will be directed to the seat or part of the room where you will sit. Sometimes you are given a sheet of instructions to read while you are waiting. Do not fill out any forms until you are told to do so; just read them and be prepared.
- Relax and prepare to listen to the instructions
- If you have any physical problem that may keep you from doing your best, be sure to tell the test administrator. If you are sick or in poor health, you really cannot do your best on the exam. You can come back and take the test some other time.

VII. AT THE TEST

The day of the test is here and you have the test booklet in your hand. The temptation to get going is very strong. Caution! There is more to success than knowing the right answers. You must know how to identify your papers and understand variations in the type of short-answer question used in this particular examination. Follow these suggestions for maximum results from your efforts:

1) Cooperate with the monitor
The test administrator has a duty to create a situation in which you can be as much at ease as possible. He will give instructions, tell you when to begin, check to see that you are marking your answer sheet correctly, and so on. He is not there to guard you, although he will see that your competitors do not take unfair advantage. He wants to help you do your best.

2) Listen to all instructions
Don't jump the gun! Wait until you understand all directions. In most civil service tests you get more time than you need to answer the questions. So don't be in a hurry.

Read each word of instructions until you clearly understand the meaning. Study the examples, listen to all announcements and follow directions. Ask questions if you do not understand what to do.

3) Identify your papers

Civil service exams are usually identified by number only. You will be assigned a number; you must not put your name on your test papers. Be sure to copy your number correctly. Since more than one exam may be given, copy your exact examination title.

4) Plan your time

Unless you are told that a test is a "speed" or "rate of work" test, speed itself is usually not important. Time enough to answer all the questions will be provided, but this does not mean that you have all day. An overall time limit has been set. Divide the total time (in minutes) by the number of questions to determine the approximate time you have for each question.

5) Do not linger over difficult questions

If you come across a difficult question, mark it with a paper clip (useful to have along) and come back to it when you have been through the booklet. One caution if you do this – be sure to skip a number on your answer sheet as well. Check often to be sure that you have not lost your place and that you are marking in the row numbered the same as the question you are answering.

6) Read the questions

Be sure you know what the question asks! Many capable people are unsuccessful because they failed to *read* the questions correctly.

7) Answer all questions

Unless you have been instructed that a penalty will be deducted for incorrect answers, it is better to guess than to omit a question.

8) Speed tests

It is often better NOT to guess on speed tests. It has been found that on timed tests people are tempted to spend the last few seconds before time is called in marking answers at random – without even reading them – in the hope of picking up a few extra points. To discourage this practice, the instructions may warn you that your score will be "corrected" for guessing. That is, a penalty will be applied. The incorrect answers will be deducted from the correct ones, or some other penalty formula will be used.

9) Review your answers

If you finish before time is called, go back to the questions you guessed or omitted to give them further thought. Review other answers if you have time.

10) Return your test materials

If you are ready to leave before others have finished or time is called, take ALL your materials to the monitor and leave quietly. Never take any test material with you. The monitor can discover whose papers are not complete, and taking a test booklet may be grounds for disqualification.

VIII. EXAMINATION TECHNIQUES

1) Read the general instructions carefully. These are usually printed on the first page of the exam booklet. As a rule, these instructions refer to the timing of the examination; the fact that you should not start work until the signal and must stop work at a signal, etc. If there are any *special* instructions, such as a choice of questions to be answered, make sure that you note this instruction carefully.

2) When you are ready to start work on the examination, that is as soon as the signal has been given, read the instructions to each question booklet, underline any key words or phrases, such as *least, best, outline, describe* and the like. In this way you will tend to answer as requested rather than discover on reviewing your paper that you *listed without describing*, that you selected the *worst* choice rather than the *best* choice, etc.

3) If the examination is of the objective or multiple-choice type – that is, each question will also give a series of possible answers: A, B, C or D, and you are called upon to select the best answer and write the letter next to that answer on your answer paper – it is advisable to start answering each question in turn. There may be anywhere from 50 to 100 such questions in the three or four hours allotted and you can see how much time would be taken if you read through all the questions before beginning to answer any. Furthermore, if you come across a question or group of questions which you know would be difficult to answer, it would undoubtedly affect your handling of all the other questions.

4) If the examination is of the essay type and contains but a few questions, it is a moot point as to whether you should read all the questions before starting to answer any one. Of course, if you are given a choice – say five out of seven and the like – then it is essential to read all the questions so you can eliminate the two that are most difficult. If, however, you are asked to answer all the questions, there may be danger in trying to answer the easiest one first because you may find that you will spend too much time on it. The best technique is to answer the first question, then proceed to the second, etc.

5) Time your answers. Before the exam begins, write down the time it started, then add the time allowed for the examination and write down the time it must be completed, then divide the time available somewhat as follows:
   - If 3-1/2 hours are allowed, that would be 210 minutes. If you have 80 objective-type questions, that would be an average of 2-1/2 minutes per question. Allow yourself no more than 2 minutes per question, or a total of 160 minutes, which will permit about 50 minutes to review.
   - If for the time allotment of 210 minutes there are 7 essay questions to answer, that would average about 30 minutes a question. Give yourself only 25 minutes per question so that you have about 35 minutes to review.

6) The most important instruction is to *read each question* and make sure you know what is wanted. The second most important instruction is to *time yourself properly* so that you answer every question. The third most

important instruction is to *answer every question*. Guess if you have to but include something for each question. Remember that you will receive no credit for a blank and will probably receive some credit if you write something in answer to an essay question. If you guess a letter – say "B" for a multiple-choice question – you may have guessed right. If you leave a blank as an answer to a multiple-choice question, the examiners may respect your feelings but it will not add a point to your score. Some exams may penalize you for wrong answers, so in such cases *only*, you may not want to guess unless you have some basis for your answer.

7) Suggestions
   a. Objective-type questions
      1. Examine the question booklet for proper sequence of pages and questions
      2. Read all instructions carefully
      3. Skip any question which seems too difficult; return to it after all other questions have been answered
      4. Apportion your time properly; do not spend too much time on any single question or group of questions
      5. Note and underline key words – *all, most, fewest, least, best, worst, same, opposite,* etc.
      6. Pay particular attention to negatives
      7. Note unusual option, e.g., unduly long, short, complex, different or similar in content to the body of the question
      8. Observe the use of "hedging" words – *probably, may, most likely,* etc.
      9. Make sure that your answer is put next to the same number as the question
      10. Do not second-guess unless you have good reason to believe the second answer is definitely more correct
      11. Cross out original answer if you decide another answer is more accurate; do not erase until you are ready to hand your paper in
      12. Answer all questions; guess unless instructed otherwise
      13. Leave time for review

   b. Essay questions
      1. Read each question carefully
      2. Determine exactly what is wanted. Underline key words or phrases.
      3. Decide on outline or paragraph answer
      4. Include many different points and elements unless asked to develop any one or two points or elements
      5. Show impartiality by giving pros and cons unless directed to select one side only
      6. Make and write down any assumptions you find necessary to answer the questions
      7. Watch your English, grammar, punctuation and choice of words
      8. Time your answers; don't crowd material

8) Answering the essay question

Most essay questions can be answered by framing the specific response around several key words or ideas. Here are a few such key words or ideas:

M's: manpower, materials, methods, money, management
P's: purpose, program, policy, plan, procedure, practice, problems, pitfalls, personnel, public relations

    a. Six basic steps in handling problems:
        1. Preliminary plan and background development
        2. Collect information, data and facts
        3. Analyze and interpret information, data and facts
        4. Analyze and develop solutions as well as make recommendations
        5. Prepare report and sell recommendations
        6. Install recommendations and follow up effectiveness

    b. Pitfalls to avoid
        1. *Taking things for granted* – A statement of the situation does not necessarily imply that each of the elements is necessarily true; for example, a complaint may be invalid and biased so that all that can be taken for granted is that a complaint has been registered
        2. *Considering only one side of a situation* – Wherever possible, indicate several alternatives and then point out the reasons you selected the best one
        3. *Failing to indicate follow up* – Whenever your answer indicates action on your part, make certain that you will take proper follow-up action to see how successful your recommendations, procedures or actions turn out to be
        4. *Taking too long in answering any single question* – Remember to time your answers properly

IX. AFTER THE TEST

Scoring procedures differ in detail among civil service jurisdictions although the general principles are the same. Whether the papers are hand-scored or graded by machine we have described, they are nearly always graded by number. That is, the person who marks the paper knows only the number – never the name – of the applicant. Not until all the papers have been graded will they be matched with names. If other tests, such as training and experience or oral interview ratings have been given, scores will be combined. Different parts of the examination usually have different weights. For example, the written test might count 60 percent of the final grade, and a rating of training and experience 40 percent. In many jurisdictions, veterans will have a certain number of points added to their grades.

After the final grade has been determined, the names are placed in grade order and an eligible list is established. There are various methods for resolving ties between those who get the same final grade – probably the most common is to place first the name of the person whose application was received first. Job offers are made from the eligible list in the order the names appear on it. You will be notified of your grade and your rank as soon as all these computations have been made. This will be done as rapidly as possible.

People who are found to meet the requirements in the announcement are called "eligibles." Their names are put on a list of eligible candidates. An eligible's chances of getting a job depend on how high he stands on this list and how fast agencies are filling jobs from the list.

When a job is to be filled from a list of eligibles, the agency asks for the names of people on the list of eligibles for that job. When the civil service commission receives this request, it sends to the agency the names of the three people highest on this list. Or, if the job to be filled has specialized requirements, the office sends the agency the names of the top three persons who meet these requirements from the general list.

The appointing officer makes a choice from among the three people whose names were sent to him. If the selected person accepts the appointment, the names of the others are put back on the list to be considered for future openings.

That is the rule in hiring from all kinds of eligible lists, whether they are for typist, carpenter, chemist, or something else. For every vacancy, the appointing officer has his choice of any one of the top three eligibles on the list. This explains why the person whose name is on top of the list sometimes does not get an appointment when some of the persons lower on the list do. If the appointing officer chooses the second or third eligible, the No. 1 eligible does not get a job at once, but stays on the list until he is appointed or the list is terminated.

X. HOW TO PASS THE INTERVIEW TEST

The examination for which you applied requires an oral interview test. You have already taken the written test and you are now being called for the interview test – the final part of the formal examination.

You may think that it is not possible to prepare for an interview test and that there are no procedures to follow during an interview. Our purpose is to point out some things you can do in advance that will help you and some good rules to follow and pitfalls to avoid while you are being interviewed.

What is an interview supposed to test?

The written examination is designed to test the technical knowledge and competence of the candidate; the oral is designed to evaluate intangible qualities, not readily measured otherwise, and to establish a list showing the relative fitness of each candidate – as measured against his competitors – for the position sought. Scoring is not on the basis of "right" and "wrong," but on a sliding scale of values ranging from "not passable" to "outstanding." As a matter of fact, it is possible to achieve a relatively low score without a single "incorrect" answer because of evident weakness in the qualities being measured.

Occasionally, an examination may consist entirely of an oral test – either an individual or a group oral. In such cases, information is sought concerning the technical knowledges and abilities of the candidate, since there has been no written examination for this purpose. More commonly, however, an oral test is used to supplement a written examination.

Who conducts interviews?

The composition of oral boards varies among different jurisdictions. In nearly all, a representative of the personnel department serves as chairman. One of the members of the board may be a representative of the department in which the candidate would work. In some cases, "outside experts" are used, and, frequently, a businessman or some other representative of the general public is asked to serve. Labor and management or other special groups may be represented. The aim is to secure the services of experts in the appropriate field.

However the board is composed, it is a good idea (and not at all improper or unethical) to ascertain in advance of the interview who the members are and what groups they represent. When you are introduced to them, you will have some idea of their backgrounds and interests, and at least you will not stutter and stammer over their names.

What should be done before the interview?

While knowledge about the board members is useful and takes some of the surprise element out of the interview, there is other preparation which is more substantive. It *is* possible to prepare for an oral interview – in several ways:

1) Keep a copy of your application and review it carefully before the interview

This may be the only document before the oral board, and the starting point of the interview. Know what education and experience you have listed there, and the sequence and dates of all of it. Sometimes the board will ask you to review the highlights of your experience for them; you should not have to hem and haw doing it.

2) Study the class specification and the examination announcement

Usually, the oral board has one or both of these to guide them. The qualities, characteristics or knowledges required by the position sought are stated in these documents. They offer valuable clues as to the nature of the oral interview. For example, if the job involves supervisory responsibilities, the announcement will usually indicate that knowledge of modern supervisory methods and the qualifications of the candidate as a supervisor will be tested. If so, you can expect such questions, frequently in the form of a hypothetical situation which you are expected to solve. NEVER go into an oral without knowledge of the duties and responsibilities of the job you seek.

3) Think through each qualification required

Try to visualize the kind of questions you would ask if you were a board member. How well could you answer them? Try especially to appraise your own knowledge and background in each area, *measured against the job sought*, and identify any areas in which you are weak. Be critical and realistic – do not flatter yourself.

4) Do some general reading in areas in which you feel you may be weak

For example, if the job involves supervision and your past experience has NOT, some general reading in supervisory methods and practices, particularly in the field of human relations, might be useful. Do NOT study agency procedures or detailed manuals. The oral board will be testing your understanding and capacity, not your memory.

5) Get a good night's sleep and watch your general health and mental attitude

You will want a clear head at the interview. Take care of a cold or any other minor ailment, and of course, no hangovers.

What should be done on the day of the interview?

Now comes the day of the interview itself. Give yourself plenty of time to get there. Plan to arrive somewhat ahead of the scheduled time, particularly if your appointment is in the fore part of the day. If a previous candidate fails to appear, the board might be ready for you a bit early. By early afternoon an oral board is almost invariably behind schedule if there are many candidates, and you may have to wait.

Take along a book or magazine to read, or your application to review, but leave any extraneous material in the waiting room when you go in for your interview. In any event, relax and compose yourself.

The matter of dress is important. The board is forming impressions about you – from your experience, your manners, your attitude, and your appearance. Give your personal appearance careful attention. Dress your best, but not your flashiest. Choose conservative, appropriate clothing, and be sure it is immaculate. This is a business interview, and your appearance should indicate that you regard it as such. Besides, being well groomed and properly dressed will help boost your confidence.

Sooner or later, someone will call your name and escort you into the interview room. *This is it.* From here on you are on your own. It is too late for any more preparation. But remember, you asked for this opportunity to prove your fitness, and you are here because your request was granted.

What happens when you go in?

The usual sequence of events will be as follows: The clerk (who is often the board stenographer) will introduce you to the chairman of the oral board, who will introduce you to the other members of the board. Acknowledge the introductions before you sit down. Do not be surprised if you find a microphone facing you or a stenotypist sitting by. Oral interviews are usually recorded in the event of an appeal or other review.

Usually the chairman of the board will open the interview by reviewing the highlights of your education and work experience from your application – primarily for the benefit of the other members of the board, as well as to get the material into the record. Do not interrupt or comment unless there is an error or significant misinterpretation; if that is the case, do not hesitate. But do not quibble about insignificant matters. Also, he will usually ask you some question about your education, experience or your present job – partly to get you to start talking and to establish the interviewing "rapport." He may start the actual questioning, or turn it over to one of the other members. Frequently, each member undertakes the questioning on a particular area, one in which he is perhaps most competent, so you can expect each member to participate in the examination. Because time is limited, you may also expect some rather abrupt switches in the direction the questioning takes, so do not be upset by it. Normally, a board member will not pursue a single line of questioning unless he discovers a particular strength or weakness.

After each member has participated, the chairman will usually ask whether any member has any further questions, then will ask you if you have anything you wish to add. Unless you are expecting this question, it may floor you. Worse, it may start you off on an extended, extemporaneous speech. The board is not usually seeking more information. The question is principally to offer you a last opportunity to present further qualifications or to indicate that you have nothing to add. So, if you feel that a significant qualification or characteristic has been overlooked, it is proper to point it out in a sentence or so. Do not compliment the board on the thoroughness of their examination – they have been sketchy, and you know it. If you wish, merely say, "No thank you, I have nothing further to add." This is a point where you can "talk yourself out" of a good impression or fail to present an important bit of information. Remember, *you close the interview yourself.*

The chairman will then say, "That is all, Mr. _____, thank you." Do not be startled; the interview is over, and quicker than you think. Thank him, gather your belongings and take your leave. Save your sigh of relief for the other side of the door.

How to put your best foot forward

Throughout this entire process, you may feel that the board individually and collectively is trying to pierce your defenses, seek out your hidden weaknesses and embarrass and confuse you. Actually, this is not true. They are obliged to make an appraisal of your qualifications for the job you are seeking, and they want to see you in your best light. Remember, they must interview all candidates and a non-cooperative candidate may become a failure in spite of their best efforts to bring out his qualifications. Here are 15 suggestions that will help you:

1) Be natural – Keep your attitude confident, not cocky

If you are not confident that you can do the job, do not expect the board to be. Do not apologize for your weaknesses, try to bring out your strong points. The board is interested in a positive, not negative, presentation. Cockiness will antagonize any board member and make him wonder if you are covering up a weakness by a false show of strength.

2) Get comfortable, but don't lounge or sprawl

Sit erectly but not stiffly. A careless posture may lead the board to conclude that you are careless in other things, or at least that you are not impressed by the importance of the occasion. Either conclusion is natural, even if incorrect. Do not fuss with your clothing, a pencil or an ashtray. Your hands may occasionally be useful to emphasize a point; do not let them become a point of distraction.

3) Do not wisecrack or make small talk

This is a serious situation, and your attitude should show that you consider it as such. Further, the time of the board is limited – they do not want to waste it, and neither should you.

4) Do not exaggerate your experience or abilities

In the first place, from information in the application or other interviews and sources, the board may know more about you than you think. Secondly, you probably will not get away with it. An experienced board is rather adept at spotting such a situation, so do not take the chance.

5) If you know a board member, do not make a point of it, yet do not hide it

Certainly you are not fooling him, and probably not the other members of the board. Do not try to take advantage of your acquaintanceship – it will probably do you little good.

6) Do not dominate the interview

Let the board do that. They will give you the clues – do not assume that you have to do all the talking. Realize that the board has a number of questions to ask you, and do not try to take up all the interview time by showing off your extensive knowledge of the answer to the first one.

7) Be attentive

You only have 20 minutes or so, and you should keep your attention at its sharpest throughout. When a member is addressing a problem or question to you, give him your undivided attention. Address your reply principally to him, but do not exclude the other board members.

8) Do not interrupt

A board member may be stating a problem for you to analyze. He will ask you a question when the time comes. Let him state the problem, and wait for the question.

9) Make sure you understand the question

Do not try to answer until you are sure what the question is. If it is not clear, restate it in your own words or ask the board member to clarify it for you. However, do not haggle about minor elements.

10) Reply promptly but not hastily

A common entry on oral board rating sheets is "candidate responded readily," or "candidate hesitated in replies." Respond as promptly and quickly as you can, but do not jump to a hasty, ill-considered answer.

11) Do not be peremptory in your answers

A brief answer is proper – but do not fire your answer back. That is a losing game from your point of view. The board member can probably ask questions much faster than you can answer them.

12) Do not try to create the answer you think the board member wants

He is interested in what kind of mind you have and how it works – not in playing games. Furthermore, he can usually spot this practice and will actually grade you down on it.

13) Do not switch sides in your reply merely to agree with a board member

Frequently, a member will take a contrary position merely to draw you out and to see if you are willing and able to defend your point of view. Do not start a debate, yet do not surrender a good position. If a position is worth taking, it is worth defending.

14) Do not be afraid to admit an error in judgment if you are shown to be wrong

The board knows that you are forced to reply without any opportunity for careful consideration. Your answer may be demonstrably wrong. If so, admit it and get on with the interview.

15) Do not dwell at length on your present job

The opening question may relate to your present assignment. Answer the question but do not go into an extended discussion. You are being examined for a *new* job, not your present one. As a matter of fact, try to phrase ALL your answers in terms of the job for which you are being examined.

Basis of Rating

Probably you will forget most of these "do's" and "don'ts" when you walk into the oral interview room. Even remembering them all will not ensure you a passing grade. Perhaps you did not have the qualifications in the first place. But remembering them will help you to put your best foot forward, without treading on the toes of the board members.

Rumor and popular opinion to the contrary notwithstanding, an oral board wants you to make the best appearance possible. They know you are under pressure – but they also want to see how you respond to it as a guide to what your reaction would be under the pressures of the job you seek. They will be influenced by the degree of poise you display, the personal traits you show and the manner in which you respond.

EXAMINATION SECTION

EXAMINATION SECTION
TEST 1

Directions: Each question or incomplete statement is followed by several suggested answers or completions. Select the one that BEST answers the question or completes the statement. *PRINT THE LETTER OF THE CORRECT ANSWER IN THE SPACE AT THE RIGHT.*

1) _____ refers to a ranger's power or right to give commands, enforce obedience, take action and make decisions.

1. _____

   A.   Jurisdiction
   B.   License
   C.   Authority
   D.   Sanction

2) The primary objective of most of a park ranger's enforcement actions is

2. _____

   A.   correction and punishment
   B.   establishing authority and control
   C.   education and information
   D.   decreasing liability

3) Which of the following ranger services is LEAST likely to be provided through visitor contact?

3. _____

   A.   Interpretive
   B.   Resource management
   C.   Safety
   D.   Search, rescue and recovery

4) A ranger comes upon a location that she believes to be a crime scene, but she has no training in criminal investigation. As the first park official on the scene, she should

4. _____

   A.   disperse everyone in the area
   B.   record existing and relevant data in a notebook
   C.   straighten or clean up the scene
   D.   interview available witnesses

5) In most automobiles, the VIN plate is on the

5. _____

   A.   driver's side doorjamb
   B.   driver's side windshield post
   C.   driver's side dashboard
   D.   passenger's side dashboard

6)   A park's "situation map" should be marked on a surface of   6. _____

A.   wood or plywood
B.   paper
C.   enamel or clear acetate
D.   canvas

7)   The Rhomberg test is a field test most useful for indicating _____   7. _____
_____ intoxication.

A.   alcohol
B.   marijuana
C.   cocaine
D.   methamphetamine

8)   A ranger on patrol should imagine his/her key responsibility to be   8. _____

A.   conservation
B.   prevention
C.   surveillance
D.   observation

9)   The form of federal jurisdiction that a park ranger will encounter most   9. _____
rarely is _____ jurisdiction, which means the federal govern-
ment has been granted the right by a state to exercise certain state authorities.

A.   partial
B.   proprietary
C.   multiple
D.   concurrent

10)   One of the actions within a park ranger's continuum of enforcement   10. _____
levels is the verbal warning. The key to issuing a verbal warning is for a park
ranger to

A.   maintain a stern and authoritative tone of voice
B.   convince the offender of the seriousness of the offense
C.   convince the offender that the warning is really just a friendly chat
D.   be certain he has the authority to implement the consequences if it
becomes necessary

11) For most park agencies, the most appropriate training vehicle for providing training to rangers who will have law enforcement authority includes a   11. _____

    I.   basic agency-wide course of 40 to 80 hours
    II.   20- to 40-hour orientation course at the assigned park
    III.   3- to 6-month on-the-job training program at the assigned park
    IV.   participation in special training courses as opportunities arise.

A.   I and II
B.   II and III
C.   II, III and IV
D.   I, II, III and IV

12) Generally, the use of vehicles for park patrol   12. _____

    I.   greatly increases a ranger's ability to respond quickly to emergencies
    II.   is the optimal method for increasing personal contact with visitors
    III.   affords the ranger a degree of protection
    IV.   offers the most efficient method of patrol with limited man power

A.   I, II and III
B.   I, III and IV
C.   II and III
D.   I, II, III and IV

13) Whenever a suitable wall surface isn't available for conducting a search of an offender, a kneeling search may be appropriate. In a standard kneeling search, the   13. _____

A.   offender's knees should be together
B.   offender's feet should be spread apart
C.   offender's hand should be raised high above his head
D.   ranger should search from behind the offender

14) When initiating communication with visitors in an enforcement situation, the ranger's most immediate responsibility is to   14. _____

A.   help the visitor understand the seriousness of the offense
B.   create a supportive rather than defensive climate
C.   make sure the visitor is aware of the ranger's authority to enforce
D.   ensure that the visitor is physically incapable of mounting an attack

15) Which of the following types of knots is used to attach a rope to the middle of another rope?

15. _____

A. Prusik
B. Clove hitch
C. Square lashing
D. Shear lashing

16) Listening is usually thought of as being accomplished on four levels. The highest level involves

16. _____

A. listening with understanding of the speaker's point of view
B. making sense out of sound
C. critically evaluating what is said
D. understanding the literal meaning of what is said

17) Which of the following structures may generally be entered unconditionally by a ranger in an enforcement situation?

17. _____

    I. Park administrative building
    II. Public restrooms
    III. Visitor abodes
    IV. Concessionaire's leased building

A. I and II
B. I, II and III
C. II and III
D. I, II, III and IV

18) Which of the following is most likely to be a standard item for a mounted patrol?

18. _____

A. Animal noose
B. Survival kit
C. Flares
D. Hydraulic jack

19) "Thumbnail" descriptions of persons include each of the following, EXCEPT

19. _____

A. Hair color
B. Eyes
C. Clothing
D. Race

20) A ranger is reading a park map grid reference. On such maps, a four-digit grid reference number refers to the grid square located to the _____ _____ the point of intersection of the lines relating to the grid numbers.

A. right and above
B. right and below
C. left and above
D. left and below

20. _____

21) It is usually permissible to search an offender incidental to an arrest. Which of the following statements about such searches is TRUE?

A. During a legal search, a ranger may seize items that are not only in actual possession, but within reach of the person at the time of the search.
B. Evidence of a crime other than the one for which the ranger has an arrest warrant is generally not seizable .
C. Stop-and-frisk searches are permitted under most situations.
D. A legal search may usually be conducted by any ranger who has arrest powers.

21. _____

22) A ranger is helping to compose the interpretive text for visitor center exhibits. The best text-on-background color combination in terms of legibility would be

A. black on white
B. green on white
C. green on red
D. blue on white

22. _____

23) Before conducting a search, a park ranger should always obtain a search warrant if there is time, or whenever there is doubt as to whether one is necessary. Generally, a search warrant is required if

A. exceptional circumstances create probable cause that contraband or other evidence will soon be destroyed
B. the search is of a motor vehicle that is capable of being moved out of the ranger's control and there is probable cause to believe that someone in the vehicle has been involved in the commission of a crime
C. the search is of a habitable dwelling on park grounds that is owned by the park, but occupied by the suspect as a camping abode
D. the search is incidental to a lawful arrest and confined to the offender's person

23. _____

24)   A ranger should consider the primary objective of a park agency's   24. _____
interpretive services to be

A.   informing
B.   dispelling commonly held assumptions
C.   furthering an agenda
D.   inciting the visitor to some action or feeling

25)   In certain circumstances, search of a person or premises may be ap-   25. _____
propriate even though legal grounds are weak or absent. Such searches may
be conducted with consent. Which of the following statements concerning
consent searches is TRUE?

A.   The person granting consent does not necessarily have to be aware of
the right to refuse consent.
B.   A consent to enter premises implies a consent to search.
C.   A statement welcoming a search implies that a warrant is not demand-
ed.
D.   Consent may be revoked at any time, but the revocation does not in-
validate any evidence seized prior to the revocation.

KEY (CORRECT ANSWERS)

1. C
2. C
3. B
4. B
5. C

6. C
7. A
8. D
9. A
10. D

11. C
12. B
13. D
14. B
15. A

16. A
17. A
18. C
19. B
20. A

21. A
22. D
23. C
24. D
25. D

TEST 2

Directions: Each question or incomplete statement is followed by several suggested answers or completions. Select the one that BEST answers the question or completes the statement. *PRINT THE LETTER OF THE CORRECT ANSWER IN THE SPACE AT THE RIGHT.*

1) In most cases it is appropriate for a park ranger to think of visitors as

1. _____

    I.   not dependent on the ranger; it is the ranger who is dependent on them

    II.   the most important people the ranger will come into contact with

    III.   not an interruption of the ranger's work, but the main reason for it

    IV.   outsiders who will alter the park, rather than an integral part of the environment

A.   I and II
B.   I, II and III
C.   II, III and IV
D.   I, II, III and IV

2) Which of following legal terms is used to denote the proof that a crime has occurred?

2. _____

A.   *Corpus delicti*
B.   *Habeus corpus*
C.   *Respondeat superior*
D.   Probable cause

3) In the continuum of a park ranger's enforcement priorities, "Priority 1" situations deal with

3. _____

A.   the protection of visitors from each other
B.   situations in which neither the park nor its visitors are in any immediate danger
C.   the protection of the park's resources from the visitor
D.   the protection of visitors from hazardous conditions created by park resources

4)   The strongest ropes are generally made of   4. _____

A.   polypropylene
B.   nylon
C.   manila
D.   Dacron

5)   A ranger is helping to compose the interpretive text for visitor center   5. _____
exhibits. For one exhibit, visitors will be about 15 feet from the text. The letters for this text should be at least _____ high.

A.   a half-inch
B.   an inch
C.   an inch-and-a-half
D.   two inches

6)   The primary purposes of patrol include   6. _____

        I.   providing resource protection
        II.   making assistance available to visitors
        III.   providing a deterrent for destructive behavior
        IV.   observing the park and visitor behavior

A.   I and II
B.   II and IV
C.   II, III and IV
D.   I, II, III and IV

7)   A ranger is one of the first officials to arrive at the scene of a crime.   7. _____
Preliminary procedures that will ordinarily be undertaken by the investigating
ranger include each of the following, EXCEPT

A.   safeguarding the area
B.   conducting a methodic crime scene search
C.   separating witnesses from bystanders and obtaining statements
D.   rendering assistance to the injured

8)   In areas of _____ jurisdiction, only state law is considered   8. _____
to be in effect, meaning that federal officers may enforce rules and regulations
only such as Title 36, CFR and other federal laws allow regardless of jurisdiction.

A.   partial
B.   proprietary
C.   concurrent
D.   exclusive

9)   To be legal, a search warrant should specifically identify the   9. _____

      I.   property to be seized
      II.   place to be searched
      III.   limits of the search
      IV.   probable cause upon which the search is based

A.   I and II
B.   II, III and IV
C.   III and IV
D.   I, II, III and IV

10)   Which of the following is a guideline that should be followed in han-   10. _____
dling a domestic dispute on park property?

A.   If the situation seems to justify the intervention of a professional coun-
selor, recommend counseling in a general way.
B.   Offer legal advice if either of the parties is considering legal action.
C.   Ask questions that will determine who is at fault or who began the
altercation.
D.   Try to stay out of such disputes unless it becomes clear that someone is
in danger of imminent physical harm.

11)   Rangers are often brought into contact with groups who represent   11. _____
"subcultures"—groups of a similar age, race, occupation or other grouping
characteristics that may lead to the development of a kind of dialect or language system all their own. In communicating with these groups—especially
in enforcement situations—it is important for the ranger to

A.   acknowledge only standard grammatical English
B.   understand the "language" of the subculture, but not to use it
C.   try to communicate with these groups using their own dialect or jargon
D.   try to speak as little as possible

12)   Rangers without law enforcement authority are empowered, in some   12. _____
situations, to

      I.   issue citations
      II.   detain visitors
      III.   search visitors
      IV.   seize property

A.   I only
B.   I and II
C.   I, II and III
D.   I, II, III and IV

13) Which of the following is a disadvantage associated with foot patrol?   13. _____

A. Ranger's presence is suggested, rather than seen or heard
B. Restricted to extensive-use areas
C. Direct contact with visitors is inhibited
D. Limited ability to respond to situations outside the immediate area

14) Guidelines for search-and-rescue operations within a park include   14. _____

    I. Radio-equipped searchers should be sent to danger or vantage points.
    II. If dogs are used, they should be on a leash.
    III. Searches should generally not be continued after dark unless a life-or-death situation exists.
    IV. Each searcher should periodically call out the name(s) of the lost person(s).

A. I and II
B. I, II and III
C. IV only
D. I, II, III and IV

15) The ability of park rangers to implement enforcement services is dependent upon a number of factors. Which of the following is LEAST likely to be one of these factors?   15. _____

A. The park agency's policies
B. The ranger's level of certainty about the appropriateness of enforcement
C. The individual ranger's level of training and expertise
D. The authority and jurisdiction authorized by law

16) Good listening skills for rangers include   16. _____

    I. Forming judgements before listening to the speaker, based on appearance and demeanor
    II. Considering listening to be an active process
    III. Always taking notes while listening
    IV. Listening to how something is being said before concentrating on the actual content of the message

A. I and II
B. II only
C. II, III and IV
D. I, II, III and IV

17)   Which of the following is NOT generally considered part of the standard frisk procedure?   17. _____

A.   Offender's feet spread about two feet apart.
B.   Offender's hands extended above the head, with fingers spread.
C.   Ranger moves fingertips over all searchable areas, crushing clothing to locate concealed weapons.
D.   Offenders considered dangerous should be handcuffed prior to the frisk.

18)   One of the signs that a person has overdosed on a stimulant is   18. _____

A.   cold, clammy skin
B.   fatigue
C.   slurred speech
D.   convulsions

19)   Which of the following is NOT a guideline that should usually be followed in conducting patrols?   19. _____

A.   Patrols should always follow the same method, route, and schedule.
B.   Patrol rangers should periodically stop at "overview" points.
C.   Open patrol is, in most situations, preferred to hidden patrol.
D.   Whenever possible, patrols should be conducted by a team of two.

20)   In relaying a description of an individual, the first detail given is usually   20. _____

A.   sex
B.   age
C.   race
D.   height

21)   Normally, searches of vehicles by a park ranger require a search warrant. Exceptions include   21. _____

        I.   whenever probable cause to search exists
        II.   the search is incidental to an arrest
        III.   items are in open view through the vehicle's window
        IV.   the vehicle has stopped at an authorized roadblock

A.   I only
B.   I and II
C.   I, II and III
D.   I, II, III and IV

22)   Which of the following is LEAST likely to be a standard item for a   22. _____
cycle patrol?

A.   Portable spotlight
B.   First aid kit
C.   Maps and brochures
D.   Folding shovel

23)   A ranger must attempt to stop a moving vehicle to implement an en-   23. _____
forcement action. While in motion, the ranger should stay within _____
_____ feet of the vehicle

A.   15 and 20
B.   25 and 40
C.   50 and 75
D.   100 and 200

24)   Research demonstrates that _____ percent of a ranger's duty   24. _____
time involves some form of communication.

A.   55-65
B.   65-75
C.   75-85
D.   85-95

25)   A ranger is called on to approach an offender who is belligerent.   25. _____
Guidelines to follow during such an encounter include

    I.   making sure that a weapon is visible and at the ready
    II.   trying to bargain with the offender for better behavior
    III.   if you do not have the authority to make an arrest, trying to
           give the impression that you do
    IV.   regardless of the provocation, never exhibiting anger or impa
           tience

A.   I only
B.   I and II
C.   IV only
D.   II, III and IV

KEY (CORRECT ANSWERS)

1. B
2. A
3. A
4. B
5. B

6. D
7. B
8. B
9. D
10. A

11. B
12. A
13. D
14. D
15. B

16. B
17. C
18. D
19. A
20. A

21. C
22. D
23. C
24. C
25. C

TEST 3

Directions: Each question or incomplete statement is followed by several suggested answers or completions. Select the one that BEST answers the question or completes the statement. *PRINT THE LETTER OF THE CORRECT ANSWER IN THE SPACE AT THE RIGHT.*

1) A ranger is composing a sketch of an accident scene. He will need to discriminate between temporary, short-lived, and long-lived evidence. Which of the following would be considered short-lived evidence?

1. _____

A. Gasoline puddles
B. Vehicle debris
C. Skid marks
D. Gouges in the pavement

2) In most situations, the best attitude for the park ranger to adopt is one that is _____-oriented.

2. _____

A. service
B. enterprise
C. task
D. staff

3) In the park setting, courts have ruled that search-and-seizure laws apply to visitor abodes (motor homes, trailers, screen canopies, rented cabins), as well as the area surrounding the abode and normally considered a part thereof (campsite, trash can, storage shed, etc.). The legal term for this surrounding area is

3. _____

A. environs
B. curtilage
C. quadrangle
D. milieu

4) Which of the following is NOT a guideline that a park ranger should use in handling a complaint?

4. _____

A. Remember that some complaints should be taken more seriously than others
B. Focus initially on the facts surrounding the situation or problem
C. Always thank the complainant for his or her interest
D. Notify the complainant when corrective action has been taken

5) Guidelines for a park ranger's enforcement actions include   5. _____

  I.   the use of physical force should be limited to the minimum
        necessary to implement the action
  II.   the vigor or severity of enforcement actions should be depen-
        dent on the attitude of the offender
  III. whenever a ranger is unable to secure cooperation, he should
        withdraw from the immediate area and seek appropriate assis-
        tance
  IV.   whenever doubt exists as to whether a situation actually con-
        stitutes a violation, or whether the suspect is in fact the perpe-
        trator, the ranger should rule in favor of the visitor and try to
        resolve the doubt

A. I and II
B. I, III and IV
C. I and IV
D. I, II, III and IV

6) A park ranger should usually think of her primary duty as   6. _____

A. assuring each park visitor a quality experience
B. enforcing the existing rules within park boundaries
C. observing visitor behaviors and being prepared for any problems that
might arise
D. protecting the park's most important resources

7) Which of the following is NOT a principle that should guide the com-   7. _____
position and delivery of interpretive services in a park?

A. Interpretation should tell the whole story, rather than just a part of it.
B. Interpretation should arouse curiosity in addition to giving facts.
C. The best interpretation sticks to information within the "comfort zone"
of visitors.
D. The best interpretation occurs through person-to-person communica-
tion.

8) _____ patrol is the method that provides the greatest   8. _____
amount of visitor access, but usually prohibits extensive observation of visitor
behavior and park conditions.

A. Cycle
B. Mounted
C. Foot
D. Vehicle

9) One of the signs that a person has overdosed on a depressant is   9. _____

A.   hallucinations
B.   slow pulse
C.   cold, clammy skin
D.   constricted pupils

10) A ranger is conducting a field interview to determine the cause of an   10. _____
incident. The ranger should know that of all the behaviors that suggest an
untruthful response, the one most commonly demonstrated by deceitful people
is

A.   bringing the hand to the head
B.   interrupting the questioner
C.   hesitation
D.   crossing the arms over the chest

11) A ranger is conducting a field interview to record a visitor's percep-   11. _____
tions of an event. In recording the visitor's account, the ranger should remember each of the following general truths about human perception, EXCEPT
that

A.   people tend to overestimate the length of verticals while underestimat-
ing the width of horizontals
B.   danger and stress cause people to underestimate duration and distance
C.   light-colored objects tend to be seen as heavier and nearer than dark
objects of the same size and distance away
D.   people usually recall actions and events better than objects

12) If a DWI suspect refuses to submit to a chemical test, many jurisdic-   12. _____
tions accept this as an admission of intoxication resulting in the revocation of
driving privileges for a period of time. This result, however, is predicated on
several criteria. Which of the following is NOT one of these criteria?

A.   The ranger has probable cause to believe the suspect is DWI.
B.   The suspect has already completed a standard field sobriety test.
C.   The ranger placed the suspect under arrest.
D.   The ranger specifically requested the suspect to submit to a chemical
test.

13) A ranger is reading a park map grid reference. On this map, the num-   13. _____
bers are read from

A.   left to right and top to bottom
B.   left to right and bottom to top
C.   right to left and top to bottom
D.   right to left and bottom to top

14)   Defensive measures consist of several levels of defense. The level   14. _____
known as "defensive opposition" involves

A.   warding off blows with limbs or a baton
B.   the use of a firearm
C.   the use of chemical irritants
D.   simply ignoring verbal and visual abuse

15)   Which of the following is NOT an element of the "legal scope" of a   15. _____
park ranger's jurisdiction?

A.   The park's physical boundaries
B.   Traffic codes
C.   Fish and game laws
D.   Criminal statutes

16)   Which of the following is an example of a "transitional" interpretive   16. _____
experience?

A.   Slide presentation
B.   Visitor center exhibit
C.   Outdoor interpretive stations
D.   Automobile tour

17)   A ranger is designing an interpretive activity for a group of elementary   17. _____
school children who are all about eight years old. For children at this age,

A.   ideas, rather than objects, are very important
B.   relations with others are based primarily on self-interest
C.   there is a strong desire for independence from adults
D.   peer relationships are very important

18)   Which of the following is most likely to be a standard item for a foot   18. _____
patrol?

A.   Jumper cables
B.   Tranquilizer gun
C.   Folding stretcher
D.   Transceiver

19)   In the continuum of a park ranger's enforcement priorities, "Priority 3"   19. _____
situations deal with

A.   the protection of visitors from hazardous conditions created by park
resources
B.   the protection of the park's resources from the visitor
C.   the protection of visitors from each other
D.   situations in which neither the park nor its visitors are in any immedi-
ate danger

20)   Recreational resources may be managed under the guidance of several   20. _____
viewpoints. The _____ viewpoint holds that resources should be
used in an essentially "as is" manner, and that visitor use should blend with
the resource base.

A.   preservationist
B.   landscape maintenance
C.   conservationist
D.   recreation activity

21)   Which of the following is NOT a guideline that should be used for the   21. _____
conduct of station duty?

A.   Whenever rangers are in conversation with visitors, they should stand.
B.   Each question should be answered as if it were the first time the ranger
has heard it.
C.   Rangers should remain sitting or standing behind a counter.
D.   Rangers should attempt to serve all visitors who need assistance.

22)   Which of the following statements about search warrants is typically   22. _____
FALSE?

A.   Searchers may remain only a sufficient length of time as is "reasonably" necessary to search for and seize the property described in the search
warrant.
B.   Generally, searchers may not seize items relating to criminal activity
that are not specifically identified in the search warrant
C.   Search warrants for the premises do not permit a search of all persons
present in the premises
D.   In most situations, real estate can be seized under a search warrant

23)   A ranger's boundary maintenance responsibilities typically include   23. _____
each of the following functions, EXCEPT

A.   physically locating the boundary line, either by previous marks or survey
B.   identifying trespass and/or encroachment
C.   marking and signing the boundary
D.   preventing erosion of coastal/shoreline boundaries

24)   The park's public relations program must   24. _____

    I.   emphasize specific stages in a process, rather than ultimate goals
    II.   solve the problems of others while solving the problems of the park
    II.   focus on challenges and shortcomings that are in need of assistance or support
    IV.   consist of actions that are coordinated and integrated

A.   I only
B.   I, II and III
C.   II and IV
D.   I, II, III and IV

25)   Arrests can normally be made by park rangers   25. _____

    I.   on an arrest warrant
    II.   on view of a felony being committed
    III.   on reasonable suspicion of a felony
    IV.   on reasonable suspicion of a misdemeanor

A.   I only
B.   I and II
C.   I, II and III
D.   I, II, III and IV

KEY (CORRECT ANSWERS)

1. C
2. A
3. B
4. A
5. B

6. A
7. C
8. C
9. C
10. A

11. B
12. B
13. B
14. A
15. A

16. D
17. D
18. D
19. B
20. C

21. C
22. D
23. D
24. C
25. C

EXAMINATION SECTION

TEST 1

DIRECTIONS: Each question or incomplete statement is followed by several suggested answers or completions. Select the one that BEST answers the question or completes the statement. *PRINT THE LETTER OF THE CORRECT ANSWER IN THE SPACE AT THE RIGHT.*

Questions 1-9

Questions 1 through 9 measure your ability to (1) determine whether statements from witnesses say essentially the same thing and (2) determine the evidence needed to make it reasonably certain that a particular conclusion is true.

1. Which of the following pairs of statements say essentially the same thing in two different ways?   1._____

   I. If you get your feet wet, you will catch a cold.
       If you catch a cold, you must have gotten your feet wet.
   II. If I am nominated, I will run for office.
       I will run for office only if I am nominated.

      A. I only
      B. I and II
      C. II only
      D. Neither I nor II

2. Which of the following pairs of statements say essentially the same thing in two different ways?   2._____

   I. The enzyme Rhopsin cannot be present if the bacterium Trilox is absent.
       Rhopsin and Trilox always appear together.
   II. A member of PENSA has an IQ of at least 175.
       A person with an IQ of less than 175 is not a member of PENSA.

      A. I only
      B. I and II
      C. II only
      D. Neither I nor II

3. Which of the following pairs of statements say essentially the same thing   3._____
   in two different ways?

   I. None of Piner High School's sophomores will be going to the prom.
       No student at Piner High School who is going to the prom is a
   sophomore.
   II. If you have 20/20 vision, you may carry a firearm.
       You may not carry a firearm unless you have 20/20 vision.

       A. I only
       B. I and II
       C. II only
       D. Neither I nor II

4. Which of the following pairs of statements say essentially the same thing   4._____
   in two different ways?

   I. If the family doesn't pay the ransom, they will never see their son
   again.
       It is necessary for the family to pay the ransom in order for them to
   see their son again.
   II. If it is raining, I am carrying an umbrella.
       If I am carrying an umbrella, it is raining.

       A. I only
       B. I and II
       C. II only
       D. Neither I nor II

5. <u>Summary of Evidence Collected to Date:</u>   5._____

   In the county's maternity wards, over the past year, only one baby was
   born who did not share a birthday with any other baby.

   <u>Prematurely Drawn Conclusion:</u> At least one baby was born on the same
   day as another baby in the county's maternity wards.

   Which of the following pieces of evidence, if any, would make it
   reasonably certain that the conclusion drawn is true?

       A. More than 365 babies were born in the county's maternity wards
           over the past year
       B. No pairs of twins were born over the past year in the county's
           maternity wards
       C. More than one baby was born in the county's maternity wards over
           the past year
       D. None of these

6. Summary of Evidence Collected to Date: 6._____

   Every claims adjustor for MetroLife drives only a Ford sedan when on the job.

   Prematurely Drawn Conclusion: A person who works for MetroLife and drives a Ford sedan is a claims adjustor.

   Which of the following pieces of evidence, if any, would make it *reasonably certain* that the conclusion drawn is true?

   A. Most people who work for MetroLife are claims adjustors
   B. Some people who work for MetroLife are not claims adjustors
   C. Most people who work for MetroLife drive Ford sedans
   D. None of these

7. Summary of Evidence Collected to Date: 7._____

   Mason will speak to Zisk if Zisk will speak to Ronaldson.

   Prematurely Drawn Conclusion: Jones will not speak to Zisk if Zisk will speak to Ronaldson

   Which of the following pieces of evidence, if any, would make it *reasonably certain* that the conclusion drawn is true?

   A. If Zisk will speak to Mason, then Ronaldson will not speak to Jones
   B. If Mason will speak to Zisk, then Jones will not speak to Zisk
   C. If Ronaldson will speak to Jones, then Jones will speak to Ronaldson
   D. None of these

8. Summary of Evidence Collected to Date: 8._____

   No blue lights on the machine are indicators for the belt drive status.

   Prematurely Drawn Conclusion: Some of the lights on the lower panel are not indicators for the belt drive status.

   Which of the following pieces of evidence, if any, would make it *reasonably certain* that the conclusion drawn is true?

   A. No lights on the machine's lower panel are blue
   B. An indicator light for the machine's belt drive status is either green or red
   C. Some lights on the machine's lower panel are blue
   D. None of these

9. <u>Summary of Evidence Collected to Date:</u> 9._____

Of the four Sweeney sisters, two are married, three have brown eyes, and three are doctors.

<u>Prematurely Drawn Conclusion:</u> Two of the Sweeney sisters are brown-eyed, married doctors.

Which of the following pieces of evidence, if any, would make it *reasonably certain* that the conclusion drawn is true?

- A. The sister who does not have brown eyes is married
- B. The sister who does not have brown eyes is not a doctor, and one who is not married is not a doctor
- C. Every Sweeney sister with brown eyes is a doctor
- D. None of these

Questions 10-14

Questions 10 through 14 refer to Map #5 and measure your ability to orient yourself within a given section of town, neighborhood or particular area. Each of the questions describes a starting point and a destination. Assume that you are driving a car in the area shown on the map accompanying the questions. Use the map as a basis for the shortest way to get from one point to another without breaking the law.

On the map, a street marked by arrows, or by arrows and the words "One Way," indicates one-way travel, and should be assumed to be one-way for the entire length, even when there are breaks or jogs in the street. EXCEPTION: A street that does not have the same name over the full length.

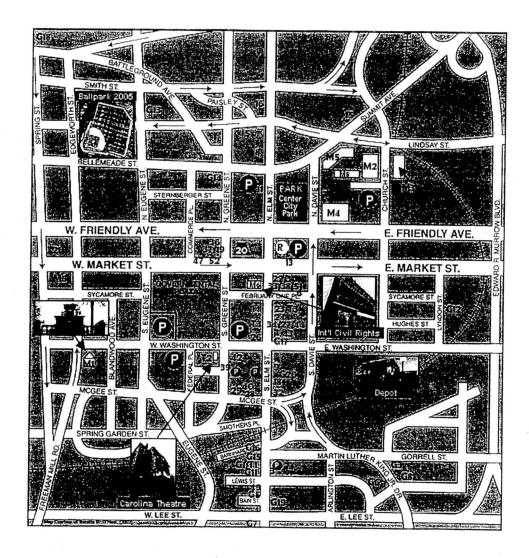

Map #5

10. The shortest legal way from the depot to Center City Park is   10._____
    - A. north on Church, west on Market, north on Elm
    - B. east on Washington, north on Edward R. Murrow Blvd., west on Friendly Ave.
    - C. west on Washington, north on Greene, east on Market, north on Davie
    - D. north on Church, west on Friendly Ave.

11. The shortest legal way from the Governmental Plaza to the ballpark is   11._____
    - A. west on Market, north on Edgeworth
    - B. west on Market, north on Eugene
    - C. north on Greene, west on Lindsay
    - D. north on Commerce Place, west on Bellemeade

12. The shortest legal way from the International Civil Rights Building to the building marked "M3" on the map is   12._____
    - A. east on February One Place, north on Davie, east on Friendly Ave., north on Church
    - B. south on Elm, west on Washington, north on Greene, east on Market, north on Church
    - C. north on Elm, east on Market, north on Church
    - D. north on Elm, east on Lindsay, south on Church

13. The shortest legal way from the ballpark to the Carolina Theatre is   13._____
    - A. east on Lindsay, south on Greene
    - B. south on Edgeworth, east on Friendly Ave., south on Greene
    - C. east on Bellemeade, south on Elm, west on Washington
    - D. south on Eugene, east on Washington

14. A car traveling north or south on Church Street may NOT go   14._____
    - A. west onto Friendly Ave.
    - B. west onto Lindsay
    - C. east onto Market
    - D. west onto Smith

Questions 15-19

Questions 15 through 19 refer to Figure #5, on the following page, and measure your ability to understand written descriptions of events. Each question presents a description of an accident or event and asks you which of the five drawings in Figure #5 BEST represents it.

In the drawings, the following symbols are used:

Moving vehicle: ⬨   Non-moving vehicle: ⬨

Pedestrian or bicyclist: •

The path and direction of travel of a vehicle or pedestrian is indicated by a solid line.

The path and direction of travel of each vehicle or pedestrian directly involved in a collision from the point of impact is indicated by a dotted line.

In the space at the right, print the letter of the drawing that best fits the descriptions written below:

15. A driver heading south on Ohio runs a red light and strikes the front of a car headed west on Grand. He glances off and leaves the roadway at the southwest corner of Grand and Ohio.

15._____

16. A driver heading east on Grand drifts into the oncoming lane as it travels through the intersection of Grand and Ohio, and strikes an oncoming car head-on.

16._____

17. A driver heading east on Grand veers into the oncoming lane, sideswipes a westbound car and overcorrects as he swerves back into his lane. He leaves the roadway near the southeast corner of Grand and Ohio.

17._____

18. A driver heading east on Grand strikes the front of a car that is traveling north on Ohio and has run a red light. After striking the front of the northbound car, the driver veers left and leaves the roadway at the northeast corner of Grand and Ohio.

18._____

19. A driver heading east on Grand is traveling above the speed limit and clips the rear end of another eastbound car. The driver then veers to the left and leaves the roadway at the northeast corner of Grand and Ohio.

19._____

FIGURE #5

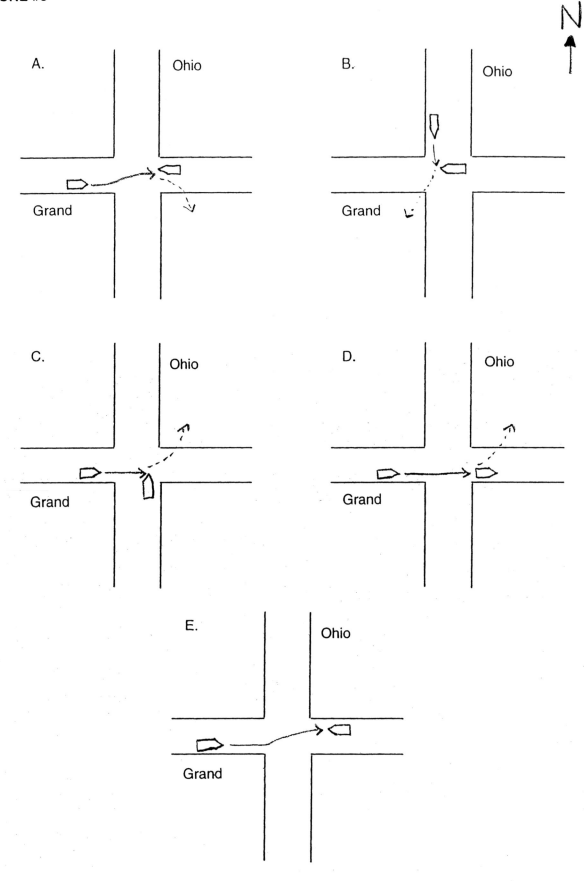

Questions 20-22

In questions 20 through 22, choose the word or phrase CLOSEST in meaning to the word or phrase printed in capital letters.

20. PETITION
     A. appeal
     B. law
     C. oath
     D. opposition

20._____

21. MALPRACTICE
     A. commission
     B. mayhem
     C. error
     D. misconduct

21._____

22. EXONERATE
     A. incriminate
     B. accuse
     C. lengthen
     D. acquit

22._____

Questions 23-25

Questions 23 through 25 measure your ability to do fieldwork-related arithmetic. Each question presents a separate arithmetic problem for you to solve.

23. Officers Lane and Bryant visited another city as part of an investigation. Because each is from a different precinct, they agree to split all expenses. With her credit card, Lane paid $70 for food and $150 for lodging. Bryant wrote checks for gas ($50) and entertainment ($40). How much does Bryant owe Lane?
     A. $65   B. $90   C. $155   D. $210

23._____

24. In a remote mountain pass, two search-and-rescue teams, one from Silverton and one from Durango, combine to look for a family that disappeared in a recent snowstorm. The combined team is composed of 20 members. Which of the following statements could NOT be true?
     A. The Durango team has a dozen members
     B. The Silverton team has only one member
     C. The Durango team has two more members than the Silverton team
     D. The Silverton team has one more member than the Durango team

24._____

25. Three people in the department share a vehicle for a period of one year. The average number of miles traveled per month by each person is 150. How many miles will be added to the car's odometer at the end of the year?
     A. 1,800   B. 2,400   C. 3,600   D. 5,400

25._____

KEY (CORRECT ANSWERS)

1. D	11. D	21. D
2. C	12. C	22. D
3. A	13. D	23. A
4. A	14. D	24. D
5. A	15. B	25. D
6. D	16. E	
7. B	17. A	
8. C	18. C	
9. B	19. D	
10. D	20. A	

TEST 2

DIRECTIONS: Each question or incomplete statement is followed by several suggested answers or completions. Select the one that BEST answers the question or completes the statement. *PRINT THE LETTER OF THE CORRECT ANSWER IN THE SPACE AT THE RIGHT.*

Questions 1-9

Questions 1 through 9 measure your ability to (1) determine whether statements from witnesses say essentially the same thing and (2) determine the evidence needed to make it reasonably certain that a particular conclusion is true.

To do well on this part of the test, you do NOT have to have a working knowledge of police procedures and techniques. Nor do you have to have any more familiarity with criminals and criminal behavior than that acquired from reading newspapers, listening to radio or watching TV. To do well in this part, you must read and reason carefully.

1. Which of the following pairs of statements say essentially the same thing in two different ways?   1._____

   I.   If there is life on Mars, we should fund NASA.
        Either there is life on Mars, or we should not fund NASA.
   II. All Eagle Scouts are teenage boys.
        All teenage boys are Eagle Scouts.

      A. I only
      B. I and II
      C. II only
      D. Neither I nor II

2. Which of the following pairs of statements say essentially the same thing in two different ways?   2._____

   I.   If that notebook is missing its front cover, it definitely belongs to Carter.
        Carter's notebook is the only one missing its front cover.
   II. If it's hot, the pool is open.
        The pool is open if it's hot.

      A. I only
      B. I and II
      C. II only
      D. Neither I nor II

3. Which of the following pairs of statements say essentially the same thing in two different ways?

3._____

   I.   Nobody who works at the mill is without benefits.
       Everyone who works at the mill has benefits.
   II. We will fund the program only if at least 100 people sign the petition.
       Either we will fund the program or at least 100 people will sign the petition.

    A. I only
    B. I and II
    C. II only
    D. Neither I nor II

4. Which of the following pairs of statements say essentially the same thing in two different ways?

4._____

   I.   If the new parts arrive, Mr. Luther's request has been answered.
       Mr. Luther requested new parts to arrive.
   II. The machine's test cycle will not run unless the operation cycle is not running.
       The machine's test cycle must be running in order for the operation cycle to run.

    A. I only
    B. I and II
    C. II only
    D. Neither I nor II

5. Summary of Evidence Collected to Date:

5._____

   I.   To become a member of the East Side Crips, a kid must be either "jumped in" or steal a squad car without getting caught.
   II. Sid, a kid on the East Side, was caught stealing a squad car.

Prematurely Drawn Conclusion: Sid did not become a member of the East Side Crips.

Which of the following pieces of evidence, if any, would make it *reasonably certain* that the conclusion drawn is true?

    A. "Jumping in" is not allowed in prison
    B. Sid was not "jumped in"
    C. Sid's stealing the squad car had nothing to do with wanting to join the East Side Crips
    D. None of these

6. <u>Summary of Evidence Collected to Date:</u>   6._____

    I.   Jones, a Precinct 8 officer, has more arrests than Smith.
    II. Smith and Watson have exactly the same number of arrests.

<u>Prematurely Drawn Conclusion:</u> Watson is not a Precinct 8 officer.

Which of the following pieces of evidence, if any, would make it *reasonably certain* that the conclusion drawn is true?

    A. All the officers in Precinct 8 have more arrests than Watson
    B. All the officers in Precinct 8 have fewer arrests than Watson
    C. Watson has fewer arrests than Jones
    D. None of these

7. <u>Summary of Evidence Collected to Date:</u>   7._____

    I.   Twenty one-dollar bills are divided among Frances, Kerry and Brian.
    II. If Kerry gives her dollar bills to Frances, then Frances will have more money than Brian.

<u>Prematurely Drawn Conclusion:</u> Frances has twelve dollars.

Which of the following pieces of evidence, if any, would make it *reasonably certain* that the conclusion drawn is true?

    A. If Brian gives his dollars to Kerry, then Kerry will have more money than Frances
    B. Brian has two dollars
    C. If Kerry gives her dollars to Brian, Brian will still have less money than Frances
    D. None of these

8. <u>Summary of Evidence Collected to Date:</u>   8._____

    I.   The street sweepers will be here at noon today.
    II. Residents on the west side of the street should move their cars before noon.

<u>Prematurely Drawn Conclusion:</u> Today is Wednesday.

Which of the following pieces of evidence, if any, would make it *reasonably certain* that the conclusion drawn is true?

    A. The street sweepers never sweep the east side of the street on Wednesday
    B. The street sweepers arrive at noon every other day
    C. There is no parking allowed on the west side of the street on Wednesday
    D. None of these

9. <u>Summary of Evidence Collected to Date:</u>   9._____

The only time the warning light comes on is when there is a power surge.

<u>Prematurely Drawn Conclusion:</u> The warning light does not come on if the air conditioner is not running.

Which of the following pieces of evidence, if any, would make it *reasonably certain* that the conclusion drawn is true?

    A. The air conditioner does not turn on if the warning light is on
    B. Sometimes a power surge is caused by the dishwasher
    C. There is only a power surge when the air conditioner turns on
    D. None of these

Questions 10-14

Questions 10 through 14 refer to Map #6 and measure your ability to orient yourself within a given section of town, neighborhood or particular area. Each of the questions describes a starting point and a destination. Assume that you are driving a car in the area shown on the map accompanying the questions. Use the map as a basis for the shortest way to get from one point to another without breaking the law.

On the map, a street marked by arrows, or by arrows and the words "One Way," indicates one-way travel, and should be assumed to be one-way for the entire length, even when there are breaks or jogs in the street. EXCEPTION: A street that does not have the same name over the full length.

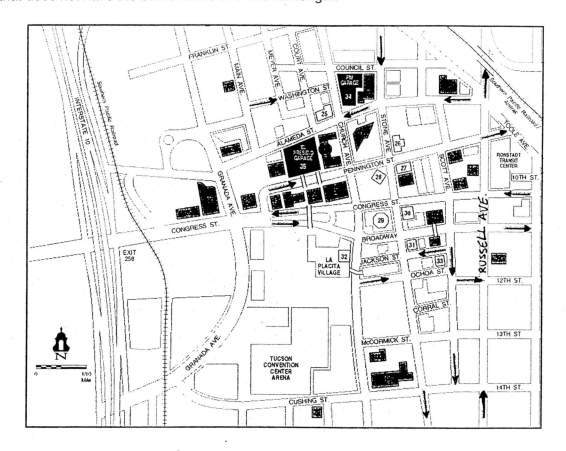

Map #6

PIMA COUNTY

1 Old Courthouse
2 Superior Court Building
3 Administration Building
4 Health and Welfare Building
5 Mechanical Building
6 Legal Services Building
7 County/City Public Works Center

CITY OF TUCSON

8 City Hall
9 City Hall Annex
10 Alameda Plaza City Court Building
11 Public Library - Main Branch
12 Tucson Water Building
13 Fire Department Headquarters
14 Police Department Building

10. The shortest legal way from the Public Library to the Alameda Plaza City   10._____
Court Building is
    A. north on Stone Ave., east on Alameda
    B. south on Stone Ave., east on Congress, north on Russell Ave.,
       west on Alameda
    C. south on Stone Ave., east on Pennington, north on Russell Ave.,
       west on Alameda
    D. south on Church Ave., east on Pennington, north on Russell Ave.,
       west on Alameda

11. The shortest legal way from City Hall to the Police Department is   11._____
    A. east on Congress, south on Scott Ave., west on 14th
    B. east on Pennington, south on Stone Ave.
    C. east on Congress, south on Stone Ave.
    D. east on Pennington, south on Church Ave.

12. The shortest legal way from the Tucson Water Building to the Legal   12._____
Service Building is
    A. south on Granada Ave., east on Congress, north to east on
       Pennington, south on Stone Ave.
    B. east on Alameda, south on Church Ave., east on Pennington,
       south on Stone Ave.
    C. north on Granada Ave., east on Washington, south on Church
       Ave., east on Pennington, south on Stone Ave.
    D. south on Granada Ave., east on Cushing, north on Stone Ave.

13. The shortest legal way from the Tucson Convention Center Arena to the   13._____
City Hall Annex is
    A. west on Cushing, north on Granada Ave., east on Congress, east
       on Broadway, north on Scott Ave.
    B. east on Cushing, north on Church Ave., east on Pennington
    C. east on Cushing, north on Russell Ave., west on Pennington
    D. east on Cushing, north on Stone Ave., east on Pennington

14. The shortest legal way from the Ronstadt Transit Center to the Fire   14._____
Department is
    A. west on Pennington , south on Stone Ave., west on McCormick
    B. west on Congress, south on Russell Ave., west on 13th
    C. west on Congress, south on Church Ave.
    D. west on Pennington, south on Church Ave.

Questions 15-19

Questions 15 through 19 refer to Figure #6, on the following page, and measure your ability to understand written descriptions of events. Each question presents a description of an accident or event and asks you which of the five drawings in Figure #6 BEST represents it.

In the drawings, the following symbols are used:

Moving vehicle: Non-moving vehicle:

Pedestrian or bicyclist:

The path and direction of travel of a vehicle or pedestrian is indicated by a solid line.

The path and direction of travel of each vehicle or pedestrian directly involved in a collision from the point of impact is indicated by a dotted line.

In the space at the right, print the letter of the drawing that best fits the descriptions written below:

15. A bicyclist heading southwest on Rose travels into the intersection, sideswipes a car that is heading east on Page, and veers right, leaving the roadway at the northwest corner of Page and Mill.

15._____

16. A driver traveling north on Mill swerves right to avoid a bicyclist that is traveling southwest on Rose. The driver strikes the rear end of a car parked on Rose. The bicyclist continues through the intersection and travels west on Page.

16._____

17. A bicyclist heading southwest on Rose travels into the intersection, sideswipes a car that is heading east on Page, and veers right, striking the rear end of a car parked in the westbound lane on Page.

17._____

18. A driver traveling east on Page swerves left to avoid a bicyclist that is traveling southwest on Rose. The driver strikes the rear end of a car parked on Mill. The bicyclist continues through the intersection and travels west on Page.

18._____

19. A bicyclist heading southwest on Rose enters the intersection and sideswipes a car that is swerving left to avoid her. The bicyclist veers left and collides with a car parked in the southbound lane on Mill. The driver of the car veers left and collides with a car parked in the northbound lane on Mill.

19._____

FIGURE #6

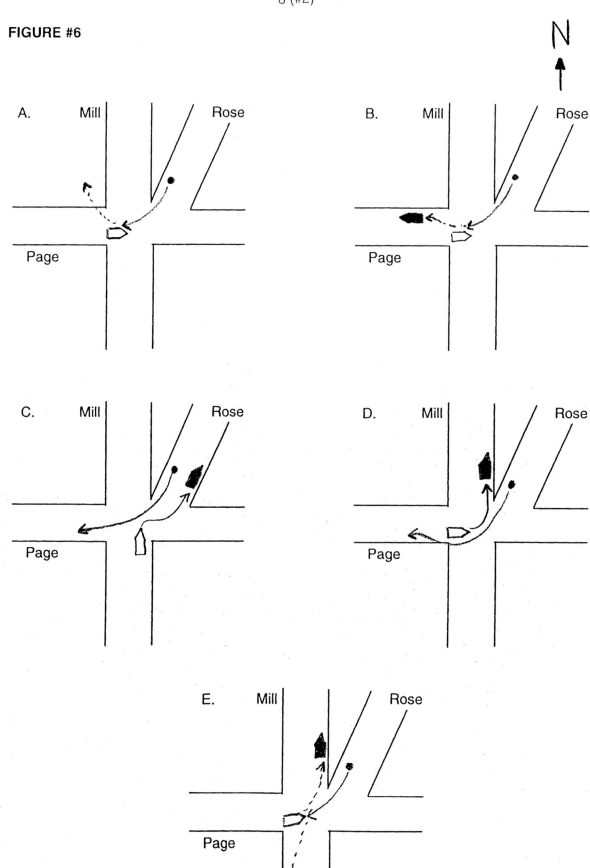

Questions 20-22

In questions 20 through 22, choose the word or phrase CLOSEST in meaning to the word or phrase printed in capital letters.

20. WAIVE
    A. cease
    B. surrender
    C. prevent
    D. die

20._____

21. DEPOSITION
    A. settlement
    B. deterioration
    C. testimony
    D. character

21._____

22. IMMUNITY
    A. exposure
    B. accusation
    C. protection
    D. exchange

22._____

Questions 23-25

Questions 23 through 25 measure your ability to do fieldwork-related arithmetic. Each question presents a separate arithmetic problem for you to solve.

23. Dean, a claims investigator, is reading a 445-page case record in his spare time at work. He has already read 157 pages. If Dean reads 24 pages a day, he should finish reading the rest of the record in _____ days.
    A. 7   B. 12   C. 19   D. 24

23._____

24. The Fire Department owns four cars. The Department of Sanitation owns twice as many cars as the Fire Department. The Department of Parks and Recreation owns one fewer car than the Department of Sanitation. The Department of Parks and Recreation is buying new tires for each of its cars. Each tire costs $100. How much is the Department of Parks and Recreation going to spend on tires?
    A. $400   B. $2,800   C. $3,200   D. $4,900

24._____

25. A dance hall is about 5,000 square feet. The local ordinance does not allow more than 50 people per every 100 square feet of commercial space. The maximum occupancy of the hall is
    A. 500   B. 2,500   C. 5,000   D. 25,000

25._____

KEY (CORRECT ANSWERS)

1. D	11. D	21. C
2. B	12. A	22. C
3. A	13. B	23. B
4. A	14. C	24. B
5. B	15. A	25. B
6. D	16. C	
7. D	17. B	
8. D	18. D	
9. C	19. E	
10. C	20. B	

EXAMINATION SECTION
TEST 1

DIRECTIONS: Each question or incomplete statement is followed by several suggested answers or completions. Select the one that BEST answers the question or completes the statement. *PRINT THE LETTER OF THE CORRECT ANSWER IN THE SPACE AT THE RIGHT.*

1. On the average, which months of the year present the GREATEST wildfire hazard due to low relative humidity?
   A. April-May
   B. June-July
   C. August-September
   D. October-November

1.___

2. To cut vegetation just above ground level, the tool MOST often used by firefighters is the
   A. round-point shovel
   B. barron tool
   C. axe
   D. brush hook

2.___

3. Using fire engines rather than aircraft would NOT be an advantage because they
   A. have less restricted access to fire sites
   B. can be used at night
   C. can carry water in varying capacities
   D. are not greatly restricted by visibility

3.___

4. On any sizable wildland fire, the LARGEST portion of suppression personnel is *usually* made up of
   A. logistics personnel
   B. hand crews
   C. air attack personnel
   D. demobilization units

4.___

5. Each of the following stages in the fire-fighting process requires sizing-up EXCEPT
   A. reception of the first call for a fire
   B. traveling to the fire site
   C. arrival at the fire site
   D. after mopping up the fire

5.___

6. The recommended MINIMUM width of a fire line constructed in brush fuels of medium density is _____ feet.
   A. 3   B. 6   C. 9   D. 12

6.___

7. Each of the following conditions is likely to *increase* the effectiveness of firefighting airtankers EXCEPT
   A. predomination of grass or light brush fuel
   B. fire incidence extending past mid-afternoon
   C. increased steepness of site topography
   D. decrease in wind movement

7.___

8. The pincer action is employed when crews attack a fire
   A. along both flanks of a fire, pushing them gradually toward the head, or front
   B. from both the front and the heel of a fire

8.___

C. along one flank of a fire to protect exposed area
D. from many points, in different directions

9. In firefighting terms, a fire's spread is considered
   moderate if its rate is
   A. of no consequence
   B. less than one mile per hour
   C. less than three miles per hour
   D. less than five miles per hour

   9.___

10. During the hottest part of the day, _____ exposures of a
    given area will USUALLY contain the highest fuel
    temperatures.
    A. north and south   B. east and west
    C. south and west   D. north and east

    10.___

11. Which of the following is NOT a danger created by late
    spring rains on grazing land?
    A. Matting of grasses close to the ground
    B. Removal of protective dust cover
    C. Leaching action in curing grasses that make them
       less palatable to livestock
    D. Increase in short-term fire risk

    11.___

12. During the day, winds on a slope will GENERALLY
    A. blow uphill
    B. blow downhill
    C. blow across the slope in one direction
    D. gust in varying directions across the slope

    12.___

13. The temperature at any given altitude at which the air
    becomes completely saturated with moisture is referred
    to as the
    A. relative humidity   B. aspect
    C. apex   D. dew point

    13.___

14. In order to adequately serve the needs of a fire crew,
    the water pump on a wildland engine should have a
    capacity of AT LEAST _____ gallons per minute.
    A. 75   B. 250   C. 500   D. 1000

    14.___

15. Usually, the MOST dangerous point from which to attack a
    wildfire directly is from
    A. uphill   B. the heel
    C. a leeward flank   D. an anchor point

    15.___

16. A *convection column* is a term referring to
    A. an inversion in the normal pattern of heat distribu-
       tion in the air
    B. a direct assault upon the head of an advancing fire
    C. a current of air rising through a fire
    D. the landward course of marine wind currents

    16.___

3 (#1)

17. Which type of cloud formation usually indicates the MOST   17.___
    adverse atmospheric conditions for firefighting?
    A. Stratus   B. Cirrus
    C. Cirrostratus   D. Cumulus

18. The effect of wildfire on soils is USUALLY   18.___
    A. a lowering of the water repellent layer
    B. combustion of mineral elements
    C. a scorched, watertight seal at ground level
    D. extraction of important soil nutrients

19. A wildfire's point of origin is referred to as its   19.___
    A. heel   B. anchor point
    C. green   D. hot spot

20. When an airtanker drops its retardant from one tank at   20.___
    a time, at widely spread intervals on the same site,
    which pattern of release is it using?
    A. Vortex   B. Burst   C. Split   D. Salvo

21. The firefighter's hand tool that is shaped like a hoe on   21.___
    one side and a rake on the other is the
    A. pulaski   B. barron tool
    C. axe   D. brush hook

22. Which of the following is NOT a disadvantage in attacking   22.___
    a wildfire directly?
    A. It exposes firefighters to flame and smoke.
    B. It results in the construction of an irregular and
       longer fire line.
    C. Normally, it does not take advantage of natural or
       manmade fire barriers.
    D. It does not eliminate fuels at the fire's edge.

23. Which of the following is NOT an advantage in clearing   23.___
    potential fire fuels by hand?
    A. Selective pruning of trees and brush
    B. Minimum disturbance of fuel break site
    C. Relatively rapid progress
    D. Leaves soil layer intact

24. In order to control a fire that is burning in an area of   24.___
    medium brush fuel, what is the APPROXIMATE guideline
    rate, in feet per hour, for the deployment of a fire line?
    A. 225   B. 300   C. 450   D. 900

25. The expansion of a fire's smoke column at higher altitudes   25.___
    is due to a widening of air currents, or
    A. convection   B. entraining
    C. subduction   D. trailing

KEY (CORRECT ANSWERS)

1. B		11. D
2. D		12. A
3. A		13. D
4. B		14. B
5. D		15. A
6. B		16. C
7. C		17. D
8. A		18. A
9. B		19. C
10. C		20. C

21. B
22. D
23. C
24. C
25. B

_____

TEST 2

DIRECTIONS: Each question or incomplete statement is followed by
              several suggested answers or completions. Select the
              one that BEST answers the question or completes the
              statement. *PRINT THE LETTER OF THE CORRECT ANSWER IN
              THE SPACE AT THE RIGHT.*

1. In timber fires, an upward-spreading burn that creates   1.___
    enough heat to advance horizontally through treetops
    without regard to the surface fire is called a(n) _____
    crown fire.
        A. passive   B. active
        C. independent   D. lateral

2. According to the National Wildfire Coordinating Group, a   2.___
    wildland fire is categorized as *large* if it consumes
    more than
        A. 30 acres of timber   B. 100 acres of brush
        C. 400 acres of woodland   D. 700 acres of grass

3. When fuel moisture is uniformly below five percent,   3.___
        A. fine fuels (grasses and brush) and heavy fuels (logs)
           burn at the same rate
        B. fine fuels burn more quickly than heavy fuels
        C. heavy fuels burn more quickly than fine fuels
        D. heavy fuels burn and spread while fine fuels
           extinguish themselves

4. Of the following ecosystem types, which one averages the   4.___
    HIGHEST frequency of naturally-occurring wildfires?
        A. Prairie   B. Dry temperate forest
        C. Desert scrub   D. Boreal forest

5. Which of the following animals is MOST likely to increase   5.___
    the likelihood of fire in a forested area?
        A. Tree-dwelling birds   B. Beaver
        C. Squirrels   D. Grazing animals

6. Generally, the SAFEST spot from which to engage in a   6.___
    direct attack on a fire site is
        A. a good distance upslope from the fire
        B. right on the fire's edge
        C. behind the fire, in already burned areas
        D. a few feet from the head of the fire

7. What is usually recommended as the MINIMUM length of hose,   7.___
    in feet, for the reels on a wildland engine?
        A. 50   B. 150   C. 300   D. 500

8. In general, the condition which is responsible for MOST   8.___
    firefighting injuries and emergencies is
        A. sudden wind shift   B. fire running upslope
        C. equipment failure   D. sudden wind shift

9. _____ action is the term for an indirect attack in which   9.___
    high fire intensity requires control lines to be
    established well in advance of the fire perimeter.
        A. Confinement   B. Flanking
        C. Protective   D. Area control

10. A scratch line is   10.___
        A. an unfinished, preliminary control line designed to
           check the fire's spread
        B. the line marking a fire's origin, usually located
           downslope from the head
        C. the systematic firebreak dug out by hand crews along
           the fire's perimeter
        D. the border between burned-out land and green
           vegetation

11. The direction in which the slope of a hill or mountain   11.___
    faces is known as its
        A. berm   B. aspect   C. inversion   D. azimuth

12. All forest fires are classified by type under the   12.___
    category Class
        A. A   B. B   C. C   D. D

13. What is cold trailing?   13.___
        A. Setting a fire in the center of a fire site to
           create a strong indraft
        B. Fighting a fire from inside the burned-out area
        C. Controlling a partly-dead fire edge to dig out and
           trench live spots
        D. Dropping an aircraft regardant payload in a contin-
           uous line over the fire site

14. What is the recommended MINIMUM width, in feet, of a   14.___
    fire line constructed in grass fuels?
        A. 3   B. 6   C. 9   D. 12

15. In order to safely set a prescribed fire, what level of   15.___
    humidity is considered to be ACCEPTABLE?
        A. 10-20%   B. 25-35%   C. 40-50%   D. 65-75%

16. In a wildfire's column, the area between the combustion   16.___
    zone and the convection zone is known as the _____ zone.
        A. smoke fallout   B. condensation convection
        C. transition   D. fuel

17. What is the firefighting term for the layer of partly   17.___
    decomposed organic material of the forest floor that lies
    beneath the litter of freshly fallen leaves, needles, and
    twigs?
        A. Slash   B. Duff   C. Eddy   D. Snag

18. The directional device used to locate fires, consisting   18.___
    of a straightedge fixed with sights, is called a(n)
       A. sextant   B. sight line
       C. alidade   D. azimuth

19. The burning pattern of an extremely violent fire, caused   19.___
    by many spot fires interacting on each other, is known
    as a(n) _____ pattern.
       A. time   B. spotty
       C. burnout   D. area ignition

20. A hand tool with an axe blade at one end and a hoe-type   20.___
    cutting edge at the other, used by firefighters to scrape
    and grub out roots, is the
       A. round-point shovel   B. Mcleod tool
       C. pulaski   D. brush hook

21. Which of the following is NOT an advantage associated   21.___
    with the use of portable pumps by firefighters?
       A. High efficiency in application of water
       B. Ability to draft water from a number of static
          sources
       C. Lightweight and easy to carry for long periods of
          time
       D. Provides access to all areas of the fire perimeter

22. When an airtanker releases its payload in an overlapping   22.___
    series from 2 to 8 tanks, a _____ pattern is being
    employed.
       A. salvo   B. trail   C. vortex   D. split

23. What is the APPROXIMATE temperature, in degrees F., at   23.___
    which woody fuels will burst into flame?
       A. 212   B. 320   C. 540   D. 920

24. The MAIN cause of irregular spread patterns in fires   24.___
    that burn in deeply sloped sites is
       A. erratic wind movements
       B. numerous natural fire barriers
       C. roll of burning debris
       D. uneven distribution of moisture

25. A break or change in the natural vegetation which might   25.___
    impede the progress of future fires is, in firefighting
    terms, called a
       A. fuel break   B. fire line
       C. firebreak   D. backfire

KEY (CORRECT ANSWERS)

1. C	6. B	11. B	16. C	21. C
2. A	7. B	12. A	17. B	22. B
3. A	8. B	13. C	18. C	23. C
4. A	9. D	14. A	19. D	24. C
5. C	10. A	15. B	20. C	25. A

EXAMINATION SECTION
TEST 1

DIRECTIONS: Each question or incomplete statement is followed by
                several suggested answers or completions. Select the
                one that BEST answers the question or completes the
                statement. *PRINT THE LETTER OF THE CORRECT ANSWER IN
                THE SPACE AT THE RIGHT.*

1. In order to control a fire that is burning in an area of   1.___
    grassy fuel, what is the APPROXIMATE guideline rate, in
    feet per hour, for the deployment of a fire line?
        A. 225   B. 300   C. 450   D. 900

2. In comparison to fine fuels such as grass and brush,   2.___
    heavy fuels, such as logs, are USUALLY
        A. wetter on the surface
        B. lower in temperature during the day
        C. drier at any given time of day
        D. lower in temperature at night

3. The burning pattern of a fast-moving fire with a well-   3.___
    defined perimeter is known as a(n) _____ pattern.
        A. time   B. spotty
        C. burnout   D. area ignition

4. For small point fires, the vehicle used MOST often by   4.___
    firefighters is the
        A. pickup pumper   B. engine
        C. aircraft   D. water tender

5. Which of the following is NOT an advantage of an indirect   5.___
    attack on a wildfire?
        A. The amount of total fire line is limited
        B. The burned area is decided beforehand according to
           a plan
        C. Reduction in the loss of resources, compared to
           other methods
        D. Mopping-up exercises are reduced

6. If the slope of a fire site doubles, the corresponding   6.___
    result in the rate of the fire's spread
        A. is cut in half
        B. remains about the same
        C. is also doubled
        D. becomes four times greater

7. In general, the TALLEST flames in any wildfire can be   7.___
    found
        A. at the heel   B. at the head
        C. on the leeward flank   D. on the windward flank

8. The transfer of heat energy from particle to particle of   8.___
   matter, by contact, is
      A. conduction   B. conflagration
      C. convection   D. envelopment

9. In firefighting terms, *report time* is the time elapsed   9.___
   from the
      A. start of the fire until its discovery
      B. discovery of the fire to the notification of the
         first person to perform work on it
      C. first work on the fire until a holding control line
         is established
      D. completion of organized mop-up until a fire is
         declared out

10. What is the term for a free-flowing prevailing wind that   10.___
    moves at an elevation where it is not influenced by
    topography?
      A. Gradient   B. Chinook   C. Gale   D. Foehn

11. A trench dug in front of a hand line is PRIMARILY used for   11.___
      A. a static water source for portable pumps
      B. prevention of leeward spot fires
      C. interception of downward-rolling burning materials
      D. emergency shelter for hand crews

12. _____ feet of 1½" hose is usually recommended as a MINIMUM   12.___
    complement to the wildland engine's equipment.
      A. 200-500   B. 500-800
      C. 800-1,000   D. 1,000-1,500

13. During situations of possible danger, the pilot of an   13.___
    airtanker can reduce risks to the ground crew by doing
    each of the following EXCEPT
      A. flying parallel with the fire line
      B. communicating the moment of drop to the ground crew
      C. remaining high until the moment of actual drop
      D. making protective drops near the crew before moving
         upslope

14. The device that gives a helicopter its widest area of   14.___
    retardant coverage is a
      A. dump tank   B. blower
      C. helitorch   D. spray boom

15. The progressive hose lay, a configuration that makes the   15.___
    most use of *tees* and *laterals*, is more likely than others
    to be used to
      A. knock down flare-ups along the fire's flanks
      B. attack the head directly
      C. control hot spots
      D. construct parallel fire lines

16. How far into the soil does the heat from an average wild-   16.___
    fire penetrate?
        A. A few centimeters   B. 6-12 inches
        C. 1-3 feet   D. 6-12 feet

17. The firefighting term for the forest debris left by   17.___
    logging, pruning, thinning, or brush cutting is
        A. duff   B. snag   C. scratch   D. slash

18. *Burning out* is a term referring to   18.___
        A. removal, by intentional burning, of unburned fuels
           inside the fire line
        B. the full suppression of a wildfire
        C. setting fires in the center of a broad fire site in
           order to create indrafts
        D. the gradual, natural process of a fire's decline
           that is not affected by firefighting efforts

19. The term for the method of determining a fire's location   19.___
    by using intersecting lines of sight from two different
    points is
        A. convection   B. indexing
        C. cross-shooting   D. inversion

20. A *holdover fire* is a type of fire   20.___
        A. caused by windblown burning material from a main fire
        B. extending beyond the predicted range of spread
        C. requiring the use of personnel from all available
           units
        D. remaining dormant for a considerable time by
           smoldering through undergrowth and vegetable soil

21. In firefighting terms, the time elapsed from the report   21.___
    of a fire to the first effective worker until the worker
    responds to the report is called _____ time.
        A. getaway   B. report   C. control   D. travel

22. To initially knock down flare-ups that occur in front of   22.___
    a hose line, the nozzle operator should apply water in a
    _____ the flare-up.
        A. stream aimed directly at
        B. narrow-angled fog aimed directly at
        C. wide-angled fog aimed directly at
        D. stream aimed slightly uphill from

23. When fuel moisture is uniformly above fifteen percent,   23.___
        A. fine fuels (grasses and brush) and heavy fuels (logs)
           burn at the same rate
        B. fine fuels burn more quickly than heavy fuels
        C. heavy fuels burn more quickly than fine fuels
        D. heavy fuels burn and spread while fine fuels extin-
           guish themselves

24. A swirl of air that is situated within the main current   24.___
    is a(n)
        A. column   B. finger   C. eddy   D. whirlwind

25. To scrape the fire line down to the level of mineral   25.___
    soils that will not burn, a firefighter MOST often uses
    the
        A. round-point shovel   B. barron tool
        C. axe   D. brush hook

———

KEY (CORRECT ANSWERS)

1. D		11. C	
2. B		12. D	
3. A		13. A	
4. A		14. D	
5. C		15. C	
6. D		16. A	
7. B		17. D	
8. A		18. A	
9. B		19. C	
10. A		20. D	

21. A
22. A
23. D
24. C
25. A

———

TEST 2

DIRECTIONS: Each question or incomplete statement is followed by several suggested answers or completions. Select the one that BEST answers the question or completes the statement. *PRINT THE LETTER OF THE CORRECT ANSWER IN THE SPACE AT THE RIGHT.*

1. The firefighting term for a standing dead tree from which the leaves and smaller branches have fallen is
   A. snag   B. slash   C. stump   D. duff

   1.___

2. An undercut line is
   A. the level beneath a fire to which heat will penetrate
   B. a line marking the minimum estimated range of a fire's spread
   C. a special type of hose used to penetrate into the bottom-most layer of fuel
   D. a fire line constructed below a fire on a slope

   2.___

3. The act of throwing mineral soil around the base of an unlighted tree stalk in order to prevent ignition is
   A. backfiring   B. banking
   C. basing   D. buildup

   3.___

4. Heavily loaded aircraft are more likely to pose a danger to hand crews than lighter ones because
   A. stronger vortex currents from their wings could cause sudden changes in fire behavior
   B. increased operating noise makes ground communication difficult
   C. the heavier craft are more likely to crash
   D. larger retardant payloads can injure hand crews if dropped directly on them

   4.___

5. When crews attack together along the line of a given flank of a fire, they are employing the method of direct assault called _____ action.
   A. flanking   B. anchor point
   C. tandem   D. envelopment

   5.___

6. Temperature inversions increase the danger of spreading fires by
   A. providing stable air at lower altitudes
   B. feeding downward-flowing air currents
   C. accelerating the rate of spread at higher altitudes
   D. drying most fuels at lower altitudes

   6.___

7. An extended, landscaped fuel break designed to protect an entire community from fire is referred to as
   A. limbed-up zone   B. greenbelt
   C. cul-de-sac   D. staging area

   7.___

8. In order to control a fire that is burning in an area of   8.___
   woodland or industry debris fuel, the APPROXIMATE guideline, in feet per hour, for the deployment of a fire line
   is
      A. 225   B. 300   C. 450   D. 900

9. When all potential fuels in a given area are exposed to   9.___
   direct sunlight, which of the following conditions is
   USUAL?
      A. Ground fuels are warmer than aerial fuels.
      B. Ground fuels are cooler than aerial fuels.
      C. Heavy fuels are warmer than fine fuels.
      D. All fuels are nearly the same temperature.

10. Which type of cloud characteristic generally indicates   10.___
    the MOST favorable conditions for fighting wildfires?
       A. Cumulus   B. Cumulonimbus
       C. Virga   D. Stratus

11. In timber fires, an upward-spreading burn that does not   11.___
    create enough heat to advance horizontally through tree-
    tops along with the surface fire is called a(n) _____
    crown fire.
       A. passive   B. active
       C. independent   D. lateral

12. In a wildfire's column, the area that divides the convec-   12.___
    tion zone and the condensation zone is called the _____
    zone.
       A. fuel   B. transition
       C. smoke fallout   D. combustion

13. The recommended MINIMUM width of a fire line constructed   13.___
    in heavy brush that is approximately six feet in height
    is _____ feet.
       A. 3   B. 6   C. 9   D. 12

14. In order to insure mobility and safety, the water tank   14.___
    on a wildland engine should NOT hold much more than
    _____ gallons.
       A. 300   B. 500   C. 700   D. 1200

15. By constructing a continuous line from five to thirty   15.___
    feet along the edge of an advancing fire, either by
    clearing or firing, crews employ the _____ method of
    indirect attack.
       A. spot firing   B. parallel
       C. burning-out   D. backfiring

16. Fire whirls, or violent, tornado-like movements of fire   16.___
    that can pick up debris and put crews in immediate danger,
    are MOST likely to occur
       A. on flat ground
       B. near the bottom of furrows and canyons
       C. on the leeward side of ridges
       D. on the windward side of ridges

17. In firefighting terms, the spread of a fire is considered   17.___
    dangerous if its rate _____ per hour.
       A. exceeds five hundred yards
       B. is at least one mile
       C. is between one and three miles
       D. exceeds three miles

18. Of the following ecosystem types, which averages the   18.___
    LOWEST frequency of naturally-burning wildfires?
       A. Alpine tundra   B. Subalpine forest
       C. Annual grassland   D. Boreal forest

19. Which of the following devices has proven to be MOST   19.___
    effective in clearing heavy fuels such as slash and
    timber?
       A. Crosscut saw   B. Chain saw
       C. Bulldozer   D. Adze

20. When an airtanker opens all its tanks to release its   20.___
    total payload at one time and place, it is using the
    _____ pattern.
       A. salvo   B. pulaski   C. trail   D. split

21. During airtanker drops, which of the following does NOT   21.___
    usually create the potential for trouble on the ground?
    The
       A. aircraft is flying high and quickly
       B. air is still and calm
       C. fire is burning in open brush or scattered timber
       D. airtanker is large or heavily loaded

22. During the night, winds on a slope will GENERALLY   22.___
       A. blow uphill
       B. blow downhill
       C. blow across the slope in one direction
       D. gust in varying directions across the slope

23. A _____ mile per hour wind velocity is considered to be   23.___
    acceptable in order to safely set a prescribed fire.
       A. 0-4   B. 4-10   C. 10-17   D. 17-22

24. Grass is the fuel in wildland fires that creates the   24.___
       A. greatest danger to ground personnel
       B. most irregular burn patterns
       C. most dramatic loss of wildlife habitat
       D. greatest spread speed for fires

25. Because of the clockwise corkscrewing of slope fire   25.___
    updrafts, the GREATEST danger of advance spot fires is
    usually
       A. in advance of the fire's head
       B. far downhill from the fire
       C. along the right flank of the fire
       D. along the left flank of the fire

KEY (CORRECT ANSWERS)

1. A		11. A	
2. D		12. C	
3. B		13. C	
4. A		14. C	
5. C		15. B	
6. C		16. C	
7. B		17. C	
8. A		18. A	
9. A		19. B	
10. D		20. A	

21. A
22. B
23. B
24. D
25. C

———

EXAMINATION SECTION

DIRECTIONS: Each question or incomplete statement is followed by several suggested answers or completions. Select the one that BEST answers the question or completes the statement. *PRINT THE LETTER OF THE CORRECT ANSWER IN THE SPACE AT THE RIGHT.*

1. Which of the following is NOT a factor contributing to   1.___
    slower evaporation rates in areas sheltered by trees?
    A. The reduced capacity of cool, moist forest air to
       absorb evaporated water
    B. The prevention of evaporation by layers of leaf mold
       on forest soil
    C. The slightly higher rainfall in forested areas
    D. Tree foliage acting as a windbreak to block the
       introduction of drier air

2. Which of the following is NOT an effect of a tree's   2.___
    competition with other trees in a forest community?
    A. Outward spreading of crowns
    B. Natural pruning of lower branches
    C. Rapid upward growth of crowns
    D. Overlap of side-branching leaves

3. The part of a tree's trunk that is no longer living is   3.___
    called
    A. sapwood   B. heartwood
    C. cambium   D. inner bark

4. Which of the following is NOT a silvicultural system for   4.___
    harvesting lumber?
    A. Localized selection   B. The strip system
    C. Two-storied seed   D. Clear-cutting

5. Solid organic products of a tree's photosynthesis USUALLY   5.___
    end up
    A. in the center of the tree
    B. in the leaves
    C. stored in the roots
    D. in the thin layer between wood and bark

6. A tree in a forest community serves the well-being of its   6.___
    neighbors in each of the following ways EXCEPT
    A. protection from wind
    B. shielding leaves from direct sunlight
    C. enriching the earth through fallen twigs and foliage
    D. keeping the surrounding air cooler in warm weather

7. Unforested watersheds are different in appearance from   7.___
   forested watersheds.
   The PRIMARY difference is that unforested watersheds
      A. are marked by furrows and canyons
      B. are less abundant in wildlife
      C. erode more slowly
      D. are more likely to contain large bodies of water

8. Which of the following is NOT one of the main requirements   8.___
   for a forest to be of the best service to humans who
   practice conservative forestry?
      A. Protection from elements such as fire and overgrazing
      B. Wide expanses of space between each tree
      C. Strong and abundant reproduction
      D. A regular supply of harvestable trees

9. Which of the following elements is NOT one of the chief   9.___
   components of wood?
      A. Nitrogen   B. Oxygen   C. Carbon   D. Hydrogen

10. The release of water vapor into the air from a tree's   10.___
    leaves is called
       A. photosynthesis   B. osmosis
       C. transpiration   D. ossification

11. In forestry terminology, which of the following   11.___
    represents the more advanced stage of growth for a tree?
       A. Small pole   B. Standard
       C. Veteran   D. Large sapling

12. Trees in a forest community compete for each of the   12.___
    following EXCEPT
       A. growing space   B. sunlight
       C. cooler air   D. water

13. The inner side of a tree's cambium layer forms   13.___
       A. wood   B. bark   C. pith   D. leaves

14. The tallest trees of any species are USUALLY found in   14.___
       A. gently sloping hillsides
       B. low-lying valley land
       C. the upper slopes of high mountains
       D. far northern latitudes

15. Which of the following negative environmental side   15.___
    effects is made possible by preserving sections of
    forest as national park land?
       A. Decrease in nationwide lumber revenue
       B. Trampling of potential germinating ground by visitors
       C. Severe pollution of forest air by visiting automo-
          biles
       D. Contamination of forest water supply

16. In contrast to conservative forestry, ordinary or destruc-   16.___
    tive forestry
    A. is practiced according to a working plan for
       harvesting a crop
    B. does not usually affect trees that are left standing
       during the harvest
    C. regards the forest as working capital that will
       provide successive crops
    D. produces higher short-term yields

17. Winged seeds are successful PRIMARILY because   17.___
    A. their whirl simulates a drilling motion that will
       help plant the seed
    B. their slow downward motion increases the possibility
       of lateral dispersion
    C. their roots are more likely to penetrate dense needle
       or leaf cover on the ground
    D. they are usually heavy enough to remain planted

18. In comparison to wood harvested from dense forest growth,   18.___
    wood from trees that are spaced widely apart tends to be
    A. harder   B. less combustible
    C. knottier   D. softer

19. The MAIN reason that forest temperatures are generally   19.___
    cooler than surrounding environments is that
    A. water contained in leaves is more difficult to warm
       than solid organic matter
    B. forests generally grow in more northern latitudes
    C. forests receive less light
    D. trees do not generate as much heat as other living
       creatures

20. The outer side of a tree's cambium layer forms   20.___
    A. leaves   B. bark   C. twigs   D. wood

21. Which of the following is NOT an element of most   21.___
    conservative foresting systems?
    A. Rules for the selection and marking of trees
    B. Ensuring future reproduction of forest trees
    C. Planting saplings in harvested areas
    D. Estimating the revenue of future yields

22. In addition to respiration through leaves, trees breathe   22.___
    through openings in the bark called
    A. ventricles   B. lenticels
    C. spiracles   D. organelles

23. If the amount of wood that grows in a healthy forest   23.___
    repeatedly exceeds the amount harvested, the EVENTUAL
    result will be
    A. a continual increase in the harvestable forest crop
    B. a supply of healthy wood that is greater than the
       current demand
    C. a dramatic change in the forest ecosystem
    D. overmature, decaying trees that are not useful to
       human purposes

4

24. Mineral constituents of a tree's organic matter   24.___
    A. are released through the leaves during photosynthesis
    B. are the primary ingredient of wood
    C. reappear as ashes when any part of the tree is
       burned
    D. are what give chlorophyll its green color

25. The act of lighting a fire that is designed to move   25.___
    against the wind toward a forest fire and compete with
    it for fuel is called
    A. creating a fire line   B. back-firing
    C. dousing   D. brush-firing

KEY (CORRECT ANSWERS)

1. C		11. C	
2. C		12. C	
3. B		13. A	
4. D		14. B	
5. D		15. B	
6. B		16. D	
7. A		17. B	
8. B		18. C	
9. A		19. A	
10. C		20. B	

21. C
22. B
23. D
24. C
25. B

EXAMINATION SECTION
TEST 1

DIRECTIONS: Each question or incomplete statement is followed by several suggested answers or completions. Select the one that BEST answers the question or completes the statement. *PRINT THE LETTER OF THE CORRECT ANSWER IN THE SPACE AT THE RIGHT.*

1. Which of the following natural resources is classified as inexhaustible/immutable, or incapable of much change or alteration through human activity?
   A. Agricultural products
   B. Atomic energy
   C. Waterpower of flowing streams
   D. Mineral resources

1.___

2. Each of the following practices is a current method for maintaining the utility of cattle grazing rangeland EXCEPT
   A. manipulating stock herds
   B. reseeding
   C. firing
   D. maintaining constant grazing pressure

2.___

3. The one of the following considered to be an ADVANTAGE of monocultural forest harvesting is
   A. superior wood quality
   B. makes use of built-in ecological balancing mechanisms
   C. allows nurturing of shade-intolerant species
   D. decreased susceptibility to fires

3.___

4. The type of soil that is BEST able to hold water is
   A. silt   B. sandy clay
   C. silty clay   D. loam

4.___

5. The practice of *chipping*, or breaking the forest harvest down into smaller particles that can be compressed into useful products, can INCREASE the forest yield by____%.
   A. 25   B. 50   C. 100   D. 200

5.___

6. The _____ industry generates the MOST revenue in the United States.
   A. steel   B. cattle
   C. textiles   D. automobile

6.___

7. Which of the following is NOT considered to be a guiding principle in the current model for conserving natural resources?
   A. Balancing individual privilege with individual responsibility
   B. Ultimate government control of conservation efforts
   C. Concentrated, singular use of particular resources
   D. Frequent inventory and projection of resource use

7.___

8. One of soil's macronutrients is   8.___
    A. cobalt   B. calcium   C. zinc   D. copper

9. Food production in the United States is currently   9.___
    hindered by all of the following factors EXCEPT the
        A. loss of farmland to land development
        B. gradually increasing average temperatures
        C. huge fossil fuel input requirement for production
        D. transfer of water to urban populations

10. The bark of trees, long discarded as useless by loggers,   10.___
    has proven to be a useful resource for all of the follow-
    ing purposes EXCEPT
        A. medical uses
        B. construction of building frames
        C. production of chemicals for tanning leather
        D. oil-well drilling compounds

11. Of the following, the one that is NOT generally considered   11.___
    to be an advantage associated with the use of organic
    fertilizers is
        A. increased rate of water release
        B. prevention of leaching
        C. improved soil structure
        D. maximum aeration of root zone

12. APPROXIMATELY _____ percent of the earth's freshwater   12.___
    supply is underground.
        A. 30   B. 50   C. 75   D. 95

13. Which of the following is NOT generally considered to be   13.___
    part of the ocean's contribution as a natural resource?
    A
        A. highway for international transport
        B. replenisher of oxygen supply through algeal photo-
           synthesis
        C. major source of important vitamins in the human diet
        D. major source of important proteins in the human diet

14. The natural resource GENERALLY considered to be inexhaus-   14.___
    tible, but whose quality can be impaired by misuse, is
        A. rangeland   B. marine fish and mammals
        C. static mineral resources D. solar energy

15. The one of the following resources that can be converted   15.___
    into methane gas by high-pressure steam heating is
        A. high-sulfur coal
        B. solid animal wastes
        C. petroleum
        D. human garbage and solid wastes

16. Given the current methods of using fossil fuels, the
    LEAST defensible (most wasteful), according to scientists,
    is   16.___
    A. synthetic or bacterial food production
    B. heating
    C. petrochemicals
    D. synthetic polymers

17. The BEST way to restore soil fertility is by   17.___
    A. organic fertilizers   B. inorganic fertilizers
    C. crop rotation   D. strip cropping

18. The MINIMUM amount of time that toxic material will
    remain in a given groundwater supply is generally   18.___
    considered to be _____ years.
    A. 10   B. 30   C. 200   D. 1,000

19. What is considered to be the MOST influential factor
    governing the occurrence and behavior of aquatic life?   19.___
    A. Availability of food   B. Availability of sunlight
    C. Availability of oxygen   D. Temperature

20. Which of the following has NOT proven to be a consequence   20.___
    involved in the use of solar energy?
    A. Toxicity of working fluids
    B. Decrease in photosynthetic rates of surrounding flora
    C. Climatic change
    D. Marine pollution

21. More than 50% of the coal that has ever been mined from   21.___
    the earth has been extracted in the last _____ years.
    A. 100   B. 50   C. 25   D. 10

22. The natural resource classified as exhaustible but renew-   22.___
    able, meaning that its permanence is dependent on how it
    is used by humans, is
    A. fossil fuels   B. wildlife species
    C. solar energy   D. soil

23. The one of the following that is NOT a limiting power   23.___
    held by the International Whaling Commission over commer-
    cial whalers is
    A. protecting certain species
    B. deciding minimum length for permissible kill
    C. protecting breeding grounds
    D. protecting calves and nursing cows

24. Which of the following is generally accepted as the MOST   24.___
    promising solution to the increasing worldwide food
    shortage?
    A. Development of more effective fertilizers
    B. Vigorous human population control
    C. More efficient pest control
    D. Decreased reliance on meat as a food source

25. The contaminants PRIMARILY responsible for the depletion   25.____
    of the earth's atmospheric ozone are
       A. carbon monoxide   B. chlorinated fluorocarbons
       C. dioxins   D. steam

_____

KEY (CORRECT ANSWERS)

1. B	11. A
2. D	12. D
3. C	13. C
4. B	14. D
5. D	15. A
6. B	16. B
7. C	17. A
8. B	18. C
9. B	19. D
10. B	20. B

21. C
22. D
23. C
24. B
25. B

_____

TEST 2

DIRECTIONS: Each question or incomplete statement is followed by several suggested answers or completions. Select the one that BEST answers the question or completes the statement. *PRINT THE LETTER OF THE CORRECT ANSWER IN THE SPACE AT THE RIGHT.*

1. Which of the following is currently the MOST promising method for the management of the earth's wildlife resources?
   A. Introduction of exotics   B. Habitat development
   C. Predator control   D. Game laws

   1.___

2. The element of American society that is MOST responsible for consuming the largest share of energy resources is
   A. industry   B. home construction
   C. transportation   D. recreation

   2.___

3. Of all the water drawn and transported for irrigation purposes in the United States, APPROXIMATELY ____ percent is eventually absorbed by the root systems of crops.
   A. 10   B. 25   C. 50   D. 75

   3.___

4. The APPROXIMATE rate at which the Mississippi River currently carries topsoil into the Gulf of Mexico is ____ tons per ____.
   A. thirty; minute   B. one hundred; minute
   C. fifteen; second   D. fifty; hour

   4.___

5. According to current projections, it will be approximately ____ years before the world's fossil fuel resources are completely exhausted, given current methods of use.
   A. thirty-five   B. fifty
   C. seventy-five   D. one hundred

   5.___

6. Each of the following is considered to be a disadvantage to monocultural systems for forest harvesting EXCEPT
   A. long harvesting rotations
   B. inefficiency in growing and harvesting large crops
   C. runoff from intensive chemical use
   D. creation of oversimplified ecosystems

   6.___

7. ____ is considered to be among soil's micronutrients.
   A. Manganese   B. Nitrate
   C. Potassium   D. Calcium

   7.___

8. In relation to the population growth of the United States, what is the increase in per capita rate energy consumption? It is increasing at about ____ rate of population growth.
   A. half the   B. the same
   C. twice the   D. five times the

   8.___

9. Which of the following is NOT considered to be a disadvantage associated with the damming of flowing streams and rivers?
   A. Decreased energy potential
   B. Increased flooding
   C. Sedimentation of reservoirs
   D. Complications with the irrigating process

9.____

10. Given the topography of most United States farmland, the one of the following which has NOT proven an efficient method for the control of soil erosion by water is
    A. contour farming   B. gully reclamation
    C. terracing   D. planting shelterbelts

10.____

11. Of the following natural resources, the one classified as a consumptively used resource, or one whose eventual exhaustion is CERTAIN given current use patterns, is
    A. gem minerals   B. freshwater fish
    C. stationary water sources D. natural gas

11.____

12. In forestry, a sustained-yield harvest program, one that produces a moderate crop that can be harvested year after year, is called
    A. silvicultural   B. clear-cutting
    C. agricultural   D. monocultural

12.____

13. Approximately _____ tons of soil are washed away ANNUALLY from the United States.
    A. fourteen million   B. fifty-five million
    C. one billion   D. three billion

13.____

14. Each of the following is considered to be a disadvantage associated with *channelization*, or the artificial widening of rivers and streams, EXCEPT
    A. loss of hardwood timber
    B. loss of wildlife habitat
    C. lowering of water table
    D. increased flood risk

14.____

15. The MOST defensible (least wasteful) use of aquifer water, according to most current scientists, is to
    A. irrigate monocultural crop systems
    B. relieve drought
    C. provide for industrial cleaning processes
    D. fill existing reservoirs

15.____

16. Given the current methods of using fossil fuels, the MOST defensible (least wasteful) one, according to scientists, is
    A. essential liquid fuels B. heating
    C. industrial purposes   D. electricity

16.____

17. The annual allotment of _____ acres of rangeland per head is considered to be universally standard for a single cattle animal's grazing.
    A. two   B. four   C. eight   D. twelve
17.___

18. APPROXIMATELY _____ percent of the extracted forest product in the United States is used for lumber.
    A. 30   B. 50   C. 70   D. 95
18.___

19. _____ is NOT considered to be an influential factor in the depletion of American soil nutrients.
    A. Cropping   B. Erosion
    C. Pesticide use   D. Fertilization
19.___

20. Which of the following is NOT considered to be a factor contributing to the decline of our freshwater fish resources?
    A. Decreasing habitat temperatures
    B. Toxic industrial waste
    C. Oxygen depletion
    D. Siltation
20.___

21. Of the following uses of a metallic natural resource, the one which is NOT generally considered to be consumptive or exhausting is
    A. zinc in galvanized iron
    B. tin in toothpaste tubes
    C. aluminum in cans and containers
    D. lead in gasoline
21.___

22. Each of the following is an effect of oil pollution on marine ecosystems EXCEPT
    A. introduction of carcinogens into food chain
    B. acceleration of photosynthetic rates
    C. concentration of chlorinated hydrocarbons
    D. immediate mortality of marine animals
22.___

23. The forestry practice of *clear-cutting* is defensively used in the
    A. old-growth firs of the Pacific Northwest
    B. oak groves throughout the Midwest
    C. sequoia groves of Northern California
    D. pine barrens of New Jersey
23.___

24. Each of the following is a factor that affects the erosion of soil by water EXCEPT
    A. volume of precipitation
    B. wind patterns
    C. topography of land
    D. type of vegetational cover
24.___

25. Which of the following is classified as an inorganic soil fertilizer?
    A. Legumes   B. Manure   C. Sewage   D. Nitrates
25.___

KEY (CORRECT ANSWERS)

1. B
2. A
3. B
4. C
5. A

6. B
7. A
8. D
9. C
10. C

11. D
12. A
13. C
14. D
15. B

16. A
17. C
18. A
19. D
20. A

21. C
22. B
23. A
24. B
25. D

EXAMINATION SECTION

DIRECTIONS: Each question or incomplete statement is followed by
several suggested answers or completions. Select the
one that BEST answers the question or completes the
statement. *PRINT THE LETTER OF THE CORRECT ANSWER
IN THE SPACE AT THE RIGHT.*

1. *Which* of the following are the *most important* hickories for   1. ___
   mass production?
     I. Shagbark   II. Mockernut   III. Butternut
    IV. Sweetnut   V. Red Nut

   The CORRECT answer is:
     A. I,IV   B. I,II,IV   C. I,II,III   D. I,IV,V
     E. II,III,IV,V

2. *What* are some of the uses for prescribed burning? It is used 2. ___
      I. as the first step in seedbed preparation
     II. to stimulate regeneration of sprouts and seedlings
    III. to create openings in dense stands of brush
    IV. to produce a slight soil sterilant effect
     V. when only crown control is required

   The CORRECT answer is:
     A. III,IV,V   B. III,IV   C. I,II,III   D. II,V
     E. All of the above

3. *Which* of the following are *most important* in determining the 3. ___
   method of seed storage?
      I. Seed characteristics   II. Time of storage
    III. Length of storage   IV. Seed quantity
     V. Climate

   The CORRECT answer is:
     A. I,II,V   B. I,III   C. II,III,V   D. I,III,IV
     E. II,III,IV,V

4. Seeds with impervious coats should be soaked in concentrated 4. ___
     A. hydrogen peroxide   B. brine solution
     C. gibberelic acid   D. sulfuric acid
     E. sodium hydroxide

5. Palatable woody vegetation is called   5. ___
     A. forage   B. mast   C. browse   D. pasturage
     E. brush

6. *Which* of the following is the MAIN requirement for a suc-   6. ___
   cessful "type conversion?"
     A. Site and plant selection
     B. Removal of nondesired cover
     C. Establishment of a desired adapted species
     D. Soil preparation
     E. Maintenance

7. What is the *most important* sondieration for rejuvenation   7. ___
   treatment projects?
      A. Treat scattered small spots or strips instead of a
         large single area
      B. Gear the amount of forage produced to the number of
         animals who will be using it
      C. Treat areas in a way that the value will be prolonged
         for a long period
      D. Treatments should be rotated so that no one is mani-
         pulated more often than once in 10-20 years
      E. Tailor the program to fit the actual needs of the tar=
         get species

8. What is the *most satisfactory* method of seed testing?   8. ___
      A. Flotation
      B. Checking the growth of the excised embryos
      C. Direct germination success
      D. Biochemical staining of embryos
      E. Measurement of enzyme activity

9. Which of the following are important to the cold stratifica- 9. ___
   tion treatment for breaking internal dormancy of seeds?
      I. A suitable moisture-retaining medium
     II. Seeds should be mixed uniformly with about one-to-three
         times their volume of the medium
    III. Containers of seeds should be subjected to below-freezing
         temperatures for 30-90 days
     IV. Freezing should be followed by cold treatment of around
         40° F. for an additional 30-45 days
      V. After treatment, seeds should be allowed to dry thoroughly
         before planting

   The CORRECT answer is:
      A. I,II   B. I,II,V   C. I,II,III,V   D. III,IV,V
      E. All of the above

10. All of the following are true of prescribed burning EXCEPT: 10. ___
      A. Backfires are recommended where the trees are small
      B. Flankfires are used under larger trees
      C. The best condition is a constant, northerly breeze of
         3-10 mph.
      D. Weather conditions should be constant for a 12-hour
         period
      E. Day burning is preferred for minimum fire intensity

11. What constitutes sleeping or roosting cover?   11. ___
      A. Vegetation offering protection from driving rains and
         snow
      B. Vegetation from which game cannot be driven by pre-
         dators
      C. A place offering shade in summer and wind protection in
         winter
      D. Grassland for some; shrubs or trees for others
      E. Shrubs and trees on knolls or ridges

12. *How* should Bitterbrush be regenerated? By   12. ___
    I. railing   II. dozing   III rolling   IV. roto-cutting
    V. pruning

    The CORRECT answer is:
    A. I,III   B. II,IV   C. I,III,V   D. III,IV,V
    E. IV,V

13. All of the following are characteristics of non-viable seeds 13. ___
    EXCEPT: They are
    A. firm   B. blind   C. filled with resin
    D. rancid   E. thin

14. *Which* of the following are TRUE of rodent predation of   14. ___
    seeds?
    I. Small plots are more vulnerable to seed-loss than
        larger plots
    II. Endrin-Arasan is used as a rodent repellent
    III. Gum-dipped gloves should be used in handling treated
        seeds
    IV. Steep slopes are less vulnerable to seed loss than
        flat plots
    V. Aluminum powder is added to the repellent as a marker
        to attract rodents

    THE CORRECT ANSWER IS:
    A. I,IV   B. II,III,V   C. I,II,III   D. I,II,IV
    E. II,III,IV,V

15. *What* is the MAIN reason for the absence of wildlife in dense15. ___
    virgin forests?
    A. There is not enough sunlight   B. There is not enough food
    C. There is little empty space
    D. There is inadequate moisture
    E. Ground cover is inadequate

16. Cover for any species *must*   16. ___
    A. provide an escape route
    B. provide adequate food for the trapped species
    C. be dense enough to prevent continued harassment from
        predators
    D. be able to attract and isolate the species
    E. be abundant enough to offset shortages in other locations

17. *What* are the requirements for chaparral-type brushfields   17. ___
    that are targeted for improvement?
    I. More than 20% of the stand should be composed of de-
        sirable browse species
    II. Slope and soil must be favorable
    III. The density of the canopy must be less than 70%
    IV. The average height of the desirable species is less
        than 5 feet
    V. The browse is unavailable or unpalatable due to the
        age of the stand

    The CORRECT answer is:
    A. I,II   B. I,II,V   C. II,IV,V   D. II,III,IV,V
    E. All of the above

3

18. What is the *major* difficulty with the flotation test for seed   18. ____
    viability?
    A. It may be injurious to seeds with thin coats
    B. Most seeds are not so heavy as water
    C. It is unreliable
    D. It is time-consuming
    E. Some seeds are permeable to water

19. What are the *principal* benefits of wildlife openings? Clearings19. ____
      I. *furnish* forage for elk,deer,grouse,etc.
     II. *help in* the harvest of elk,deer,and grouse
    III. *provide* nesting sites for turkeys and grouse
     IV. *attract* insects that young birds need for food
      V. *offer* protection from predation

    The CORRECT answer is:
      A. I,III,IV   B. I,II,IV   C. I,III,V   D. II,IV
      E. I,III,IV,V

20. *Which* of the following factors that influence wildlife popula- 20. ____
    tions are the MOST important?
      I. Availability of food
     II. Abundance and effectiveness of predatory species
    III. Competition with other species
     IV. Disease
      V. Presence of cover

    The CORRECT answer is:
      A. I,II   B. I,IV   C. I,V   D. I,II,IV   E. I,III,IV

21. What areas should be *excluded* from any sagebrush control pro-   21. ____
    jects?   Areas
      I. of low,sparse sagebrush with a good understory of
         grass and herbs
     II. rarely used by grouse for food or nesting
    III. of low improvement potential
     IV. adjacent to aspen or willows
      V. outside one quarter mile of strutting grounds

    The CORRECT answer is:
      A. I,II,III   B. I,III,IV   C. III,IV,V   D. II,IV,V
      E. All of the above

22. Browseways and openings in chaparrel-type   brushfields are   22. ____
    constructed by all of the following ways EXCEPT:
      A. With dozers   B. With mowers   C. With rollers
      D. With herbicides   E. By prescribed burning

23. All of the following are *true* of direct germination tests   23. ____
    EXCEPT:
      A. Enough water is poured into the container so that the
         medium will absorb its capacity
      B. Temperatures should be kept constant
      C. Moisture levels should be kept constant
      D. Flats should never have watertight bottoms
      E. Light is not necessary

24. A protective cover of vegetation provides wildlife with _____ cover.   24. ___
    I. winter   II. refuge   III. loafing
    IV. fawning or nesting   V. sleeping or roosting

    The CORRECT answer is:
    A. I,II   B. III,IV,V   C. II,V   D. I,III,IV
    E. All of the above

25. When overpopulations of game exist, *what* is the FIRST step   25. ___
    that should be taken?
    A. Provide additional food supplies not native to the area
    B. Encourage natural reproduction of food plants native to
       the area
    C. Cut down the numbers of game
    D. Provide additional food supplies of the type found in
       the area
    E. The area should be made unavailable to other wildlife

26. *Which* of the following are guidelines used in juniper-   26. ___
    pinyon clearing projects in order to avoid damage to
    deer and elk habitat?
     I. Leave woody vegetation covering no more than 15% of
        the treated area
    II. Leave live juniper crowns covering 5% of the treated
        area
   III. Do not use control methods which tend to kill deer
        bowse plants
    IV. Treat slopes steeper than 15%
     V. Do not treat northerly exposures

    The CORRECT answer is:
    A. I,II,IV   B. I,II,III   C. III,V   D. II,III,V
    E. I,II,III,IV

27. *What* is the MOST important *first* step in establishing herba-27. ___
    ceous plants?
    A. Timing the seeding
    B. Getting a good cover of seed
    C. Eliminating undesirable competing vegetation
    D. Planting the seeds at the proper depth
    E. Species selection

28. Seeds with seedcoat dormancy that have been successfully   28. ___
    treated appear
    A. glossy   B. pitted   C. shriveled   D. dull   E. moldy

29. The term *escape cover* generally applies to _____ cover.   29. ___
    I. winter   II. refuge   III. loafing
    IV. fawning or nesting   B. steep or roosting

    The CORRECT answer is:
    A. I,II   B. II,IV,V   C. II,V   D. II,IV
    E. II,III,V

5

30. What is the MOST successful way of reducing herds of big   30. ___
    game?
    A. Eventual starvation from inadequate food supplies
    B. Driving the animals away from concentration areas
    C. Trapping surpluses and removing the animals to under-
       populated. areas
    D. Extending the hunting privileges in heavily populated
       areas
    E. Euthanasia

31. Cover height of herbaceous ground cover is GREATEST for: 31. ___
    A. Hungarian partridge   B. Sharptail grouse
    C. Bobwhite quail   D. Sage grouse
    E. Prairie chicken

32. What is the BEST way to prepare a seedbed for herbaceous   31. ___
    plants? By
    A. burning the site prior to planting
    B. rolling the area with a heavy log or with rubber tires
    C. scalping the site
    D. discing the soil
    E. fertilizing the soil

33. Which of the following are methods to overcome seedcoat   32. ___
    dormancy?
      I. Acid treatment   II. Cold stratification
    III. Warm, followed by cold stratification
     IV. Mechanical stratification
      V. Hotwater treatment

    The CORRECT answer is:
    A. I,III,V   B. I,IV   C. I,IV,V   D. II,III,IV
    E. II,III,V

34. Corridors are used by wildlife for   33. ___
      I. shade   II. shelter   III. loafing cover
     IV. fawning or nesting cover   V. sleep or roosting cover

    The CORRECT answer is:
    A. I,II   B. II,IV,V   C. II,V   D. II,IV   E. II,III,V

35. Which of the following are TRUE of forest openings?   34. ___
      I. Cultivated openings find their value in concentrating
         wildlife during restrocking
     II. Natural openings provide the ecological environment
         under which native game thrive
    III. Cultivated openings must be maintained to prevent re-
         invasion by undesirable plants
     IV. Natural openings are maintained as areas of annual food
         patch plantings
      V. Cultivated openings should include low ground-cover type
         vegetation and shrubs and trees

    The CORRECT answer is:
    A. I,II,V   B. I,II,III   C. III,IV,V   D. II,III,IV
    E. II,III,IV,V

6

36. Den formation is *most directly* due to   36. ___
    A. the activities of the animal user
    B. decay
    C. the efforts of birds
    D. fortuitous circumstances
    E. the activities of man

37. *Which* of the following should guide grain plantings for   37. ___
    upland game?
     I. Plots should be irregularly shaped
    II. Plots should be located adjacent to good cover
   III. Plots should be located on steep slopes planted in
         narrow strips
    IV. Food should be available in late fall to early winter
     V. Plant every year until the grain is fully established

    The CORRECT answer is:
     A. I,II   B. I,II,III   C. I,III   D. I,IV,V
     E. I,II,IV,V

38. *Which* of the following are TRUE of internal dormancy of   38. ___
    seeds?
     I. It is the most common type of seed dormancy
    II. Germination cannot begin until there are chemical
         changes in the stored food or embryo
   III. Seeds must be tested to determine the proper corrective
         method
    IV. Unusually small embryos must be given time to grow be-
         fore germination is possible
     V. Most embryos do not develop due to lack of water and
         oxygen

    The CORRECT answer is:
     A. I,III,IV   B. I,II,IV   C. I,IV,V   D. II,IV,V
     E. IV,V

39. Den trees are used for   39. ___
     I. nesting   II. brooding, rearing   III. hibernation
    IV. shelter from the elements   V. seclusion from predators
    The CORRECT answer is:
     A. I,II   B. II,III   C. I,II,III   D. I,II,III,V
     E. All of the above

40. *What* MAINLY determines the number and size of forest open-   40. ___
    ings? The
     I. presence of predators
    II. habits of the target wildlife species
   III. size of the wildlife population
    IV. stand density encountered throughout the range
     V. age and size of the stand

    The CORRECT answer is:
     A. I,II   B. II,III   C. I,II,III   D. I,II,III,IV
     E. II,IV

41. All of the following require den trees EXCEPT: 41. ___
    A. Gray and fox squirrels   B. Bluebird
    C. Raccoon   D. Bobwhite quail
    E. Owls

7

42. *Which* of the following grains are valuable for waterfowl,   42. ___
especially where the site is flooded for part of the year?
    I. Rye   II. Buckwheat   III. Millet   IV. Barley
    V. Sorghum

The CORRECT answer is:
    A. I,III,V   B. I,II,IV   C. I,III,IV   D. II,III,IV
    E. III,V

43. *What* is the MOST common method of pre-treating seeds with   43. ___
impervious coats?
    A. Acid treatment   B. Mechanical stratification
    C. Hotwater treatment   D. Cold stratification
    E. Water, followed by cold stratification

44. *What* is the PRIMARY advantage of nest boxes? They   44. ___
    A. are economical to build and to maintain
    B. quickly correct den scarcities
    C. are predation-proof
    D. are designed to meet the target species specifications
    E. increase the population of the target species

45. *Which* of the following are considered to be *type conver-*   45. ___
sions of existing cover?
    I. Creation of a permanent treeless opening in a forest
   II. Large brush fields converted to tree plantations
  III. Browse release over a designated area
   IV. Rejuvenation treatments
    V. Modification of the forest composition

The CORRECT answer is:
    A. I,II,V   B. I,II,III,V   C. I,II   D. III,IV,V
    E. All of the above

46. *Which* of the following volunteer vegetation around pothole   46. ___
has duck food value?
    I. Horsetail   II. Bindweed   III. Bulrush
   IV. Bluejoint grass   V. Marsh cinquefoil

The CORRECT answer is:
    A. I,IV,V   B. I,IV   C. II,III   D. II,III,IV
    E. II,III,IV,V

47. *What* environment is BEST for *most* seed storage?   47. ___
    A. Low moisture content and low temperatures
    B. low moisture content and high temperatures
    C. Ordinary air temperature in dry climates
    D. High moisture content and cold temperatures
    E. Temperatures below freezing

48. *What* is the MOST widely used method of breaking internal   48. ___
formancy?
    A. Acid treatment   B. Mechanical stratification
    C. Hotwater treatment   D. Chemical treatment
    E. Cold stratification

49. *What* are the *basic* requirements of wood duck nest boxes? 49. ___
    I. The opening is large enough
   II. Protection from predators
  III. The base will hold a clutch of eggs
   IV. The box is weatherproof
    V. There is enough debris to form a base and cover
       for the first few eggs

The CORRECT answer is:
    A. I,II   B. I,III,IV   C. I,II,III   D. I,III,V
    E. All of the above

50. *What* are the purposes of *type conversions* of existing 50. ___
cover? To
    I. *create* favorable interspersions of food and cover
   II. *attract* a target species
  III. *lessen* or *eliminate* predation
   IV. *develop* edge
    V. *provide* openings with herbaceous vegetation in ex-
       tensive areas of dense brush or timber

The CORRECT answer is:
    A. I,IV,V   B. II,III   C. I,II,III   D. I,II,V
    E. I,II,III,V

KEY (CORRECT ANSWERS)

1.	C	11.	E	21.	B	31.	D	41.	D
2.	C	12.	D	22.	E	32.	D	42.	D
3.	B	13.	A	23.	B	33.	C	43.	A
4.	D	14.	C	24.	A	34.	A	44.	B
5.	C	15.	B	25.	C	35.	B	45.	C
6.	A	16.	C	26.	D	36.	B	46.	C
7.	E	17.	B	27.	C	37.	A	47.	A
8.	C	18.	C	28.	D	38.	B	48.	E
9.	A	19.	B	29.	A	39.	E	49.	D
10.	E	20.	C	30.	D	40.	E	50.	A

9

WORD MEANING

COMMENTARY

DESCRIPTION OF THE TEST

On many examinations, you will have questions about the meaning
of words, or vocabulary.

In this type of question, you have to state what a word or phrase
means. (A phrase is a group of words.) This word or phrase is in
CAPITAL letters in a sentence. You are also given for each question
five other words or groups of words - lettered A, B, C, D, and E -
as possible answers. One of these words or groups of words means
the same as the word or group of words in CAPITAL letters. Only
one is right. You are to pick out the one that is right and select
the letter of your answer.

HINTS FOR ANSWERING WORD-MEANING QUESTIONS

Read each question carefully.

Choose the best answer of the five choices, even though it is
not the word you might use yourself.

Answer first those that you know. Then do the others.

If you know that some of the suggested answers are not right,
pay no more attention to them.

Be sure that you have selected an answer for every question,
even if you have to guess.

SAMPLE QUESTIONS

DIRECTIONS: For the following questions, select the word or group of
words lettered A, B, C, D, or E that means *MOST NEARLY*
the same as the word in capital letters. Indicate the
letter of the *CORRECT* answer for each question.

SAMPLE QUESTIONS 1 AND 2

1. The letter was SHORT. SHORT means *most nearly*
   A. tall   B. wide   C. brief   D. heavy   E. dark
   EXPLANATION
   SHORT is a word you have used to describe something that is
   small, or not long, or little, etc. Therefore, you would not
   have to spend much time figuring out the right answer. You
   would choose C. brief.
2. The young man is VIGOROUS. VIGOROUS means *most nearly*
   A. serious B. reliable C. courageous D. strong E. talented
   EXPLANATION
   VIGOROUS is a word that you have probably used yourself or read
   somewhere. It carries with it the idea of being active, full of
   pep, etc. Which one of the five choices comes closest to meaning
   that? Certainly not A. serious, B. reliable, or E. talented;
   C. courageous - maybe, D. strong - maybe. But between courageous
   or strong, you would have to agree that strong is the better choice.
   Therefore, you would choose D. strong.

WORD MEANING
EXAMINATION SECTION
TEST 1

DIRECTIONS : For the following questions, select the word or group of words lettered A, B, C, D, or E that means MOST NEARLY the same as the word in capital letters. *PRINT THE LETTER OF THE CORRECT ANSWER IN THE SPACE AT THE RIGHT.*

1. The CONFLAGRATION spread throughout the entire city.   1.____

    A. hostilities   B. confusion   C. rumor   D. epidemic   E. fire

2. The firemen PURGED the gas tank after emptying its contents.   2.____

    A. sealed   B. punctured   C. exposed   D. cleansed   E. buried

3. Rules must be applied with DISCRETION.   3.____

    A. impartiality   B. judgment   C. severity
    D. patience   E. consistency

4. The officer and his men ASCENDED the stairs as rapidly as they could.   4.____

    A. went up   B. washed down   C. chopped
    D. shored up   E. inspected

5. The store's refusal to accept delivery of the merchandise was a violation of the   5.____
EXPRESS provisions of the contract.

    A. clear   B. implied
    C. penalty   D. disputed
    E. complicated

6. Mr. Walsh could not attend the luncheon because he had a PRIOR appointment.   6.____

    A. conflicting   B. official   C. previous
    D. important   E. subsequent

7. The time allowed to complete the task was not ADEQUATE.   7.____

    A. long   B. enough   C. excessive   D. required   E. stated

8. The investigation unit began an EXTENSIVE search for the information.   8.____

    A. complicated   B. superficial   C. thorough
    D. leisurely   E. cursory

9. The secretary answered the telephone in a COURTEOUS manner.   9.____

    A. businesslike   B. friendly
    C. formal   D. gruff
    E. polite

10. The RECIPIENT of the money checked the total amount.   10.__

    A. receiver   B. carrier   C. borrower   D. giver   E. sender

11. The College offered a variety of SEMINARS to upperclassmen.   11.__

    A. reading courses with no formal supervision
    B. study courses for small groups of students engaged in research under a teacher
    C. guidance conferences with grade advisors
    D. work experience in different occupational fields
    E. luncheon discussions

12. The Dean pointed out that the FOCUS of the study was not clear.   12.__

    A. end   B. objective   C. follow-up   D. location   E. basis

13. The faculty of the Anthropology Department agreed that the departmental program was   13.__
DEFICIENT.

    A. excellent   B. inadequate C. demanding D. sufficient   E. dilatory

14. The secretary was asked to type a rough draft of a course SYLLABUS.   14.__

    A. directory of departments and services B. examination schedule
    C. outline of a course of study   D. rules and regulations
    E. schedule of meetings

15. There is an item in a painting contract relating to INSOLVENCY.   15.__

    A. the improper mixing of paint
    B. the use of improper materials
    C. taking excessive time to complete the contract
    D. bankruptcy
    E. the use of water

KEY (CORRECT ANSWERS)

1.	E	6.	C	11.	B
2.	D	7.	B	12.	B
3.	B	8.	C	13.	B
4.	A	9.	E	14.	C
5.	A	10.	A	15.	D

TEST 2

DIRECTIONS : For the following questions, select the word or group of words lettered A, B, C, D, or E that means MOST NEARLY the same as the word in capital letters. *PRINT THE LETTER OF THE CORRECT ANSWER IN THE SPACE AT THE RIGHT.*

1. The number of applicants exceeded the ANTICIPATED figure.   1._____

    A. expected   B. required   C. revised   D. necessary   E. hoped-for

2. The clerk was told to COLLATE the pages of the report.   2._____

    A. destroy   B. edit   C. correct   D. assemble   E. fasten

3. Mr. Jones is not AUTHORIZED to release the information.   3._____

    A. inclined   B. pleased   C. permitted   D. trained   E. expected

4. The secretary chose an APPROPRIATE office for the meeting.   4._____

    A. empty   B. decorated
    C. nearby   D. suitable
    E. inexpensive

5. The employee performs a COMPLEX set of tasks each day.   5._____

    A. difficult   B. important   C. pleasant   D. large   E. secret

6. The foreman INVESTIGATED the sewer to see whether it was clogged.   6._____

    A. compelled   B. diverted   C. opened   D. improved   E. examined

7. The foreman SUPERVISED the work closely.   7._____

    A. criticized   B. neglected
    C. praised   D. superintended
    E. reviewed

8. ILLICIT connections are often found during sewer inspections.   8._____

    A. damaged   B. legal   C. poor   D. unlawful   E. clogged

9. The sewage in the manhole was floating SLUGGISHLY.   9._____

    A. buoyantly   B. odiferously   C. slowly   D. swiftly   E. evenly

10. It is most COMMON to find sewer pipes made of either clay or concrete.   10._____

    A. characteristic   B. inordinate   C. prevalent
    D. retiring   E. vulgar

11. He needed public assistance because he was INCAPACITATED.   11._____

    A. uneducated   B. unreliable   C. uncooperative
    D. discharged   E. disabled

12. The caseworker explained to the client that signing the document was COMPULSORY. 12.__

   A. temporary
   C. different
   E. usual
   B. required
   D. comprehensive

13. The woman's actions did not JEOPARDIZE her eligibility for benefits. 13.__

   A. delay   B. reinforce   C. determine   D. endanger   E. enhance

14. The material is PUTRESCIBLE. 14.__

   A. compacted
   D. liable to rot
   B. liable to burn
   E. liable to clog
   C. heavy

15. Older incinerator plants are handstoked and fed INTERMITTENTLY. 15.__

   A. constantly
   D. with a shovel
   B. heavily
   E. every few minutes
   C. periodically

KEY (CORRECT ANSWERS)

1.	A	6.	E	11.	E
2.	D	7.	D	12.	B
3.	C	8.	D	13.	D
4.	D	9.	C	14.	D
5.	A	10.	C	15.	C

TEST 3

DIRECTIONS : For the following questions, select the word or group of words lettered A, B, C, D, or E that means MOST NEARLY the same as the word in capital letters. *PRINT THE LETTER OF THE CORRECT ANSWER IN THE SPACE AT THE RIGHT.*

1. The foreman made an ABSURD remark.   1.____

    A. misleading   B. ridiculous   C. unfair   D. wicked   E. artful

2. The electrician was ADEPT at his job.   2.____

    A. co-operative   B. developed
    C. diligent   D. skilled
    E. inept

3. The foreman stated that the condition was GENERAL.   3.____

    A. artificial   B. prevalent   C. timely   D. transient   E. likely

4. The asphalt worker engages in a HAZARDOUS job.   4.____

    A. absorbing   B. dangerous   C. demanding
    D. difficult   E. uninteresting

5. The foreman made a TRIVIAL mistake.   5.____

    A. accidental   B. dangerous
    C. obvious   D. serious
    E. unimportant

6. No DEVIATION from the specifications will be allowed unless the same has been previ-   6.____
   ously authorized by the engineer.

    A. violation   B. variation   C. complete change
    D. authorized change   E. inference

7. The contractor shall SAFEGUARD all points, stakes, grade marks, monuments, and   7.____
   bench marks, made or established on or near the line of the work.

    A. watch closely   B. guard against theft
    C. prevent damage to   D. replace
    E. control

8. Bitumen-sand bed shall consist of sand with cut-back asphalt COMBINED in definite pro- 8.____
   portions by weight.

    A. together   B. mixed   C. added   D. placed   E. undiluted

9. The material was quite DESICCATED.   9.____

    A. hard   B. dangerous   C. soft   D. spongy   E. dry

10. Malice was PATENT in all of his remarks.   10.____

    A. elevated   B. evident   C. threatening D. foreign   E. implicit

11. A Chaplain shall have the COMPARABLE rank of Inspector.   11.___

    A. false   B. superior   C. equal   D. presumed E. ordinary

12. Pushcarts and DERELICT automobiles shall be delivered to the bureau of incum-   12.___
brances.

    A. dilapidated   B. abandoned   C. delinquent
    D. contraband   E. unusable

13. When the EXIGENCIES of the service shall so require, a captain may assign a patrol-   13.___
man from the outgoing platoon to house duty.

    A. needs   B. conveniences
    C. changes   D. increases
    E. exits

14. There is a provision for the award of a medal for merit for an act of outstanding bravery,   14.___
performed in the line of duty, at IMMINENT personal hazard of life.

    A. impending B. inherent   C. certain   D. great   E. eminent

15. A member of the department shall not communicate with a railroad company for the pur-   15.___
pose of EXPEDITING the issue of a transportation pass,

    A. extorting   B. procuring   C. demanding
    D. hastening   E. extending

KEY (CORRECT ANSWERS)

1.	B	6.	B	11.	C
2.	D	7.	C	12.	B
3.	B	8.	B	13.	A
4.	B	9.	E	14.	A
5.	E	10.	B	15.	D

TEST 4

DIRECTIONS : For the following questions, select the word or group of words lettered A, B, C, D, or E that means MOST NEARLY the same as the word in capital letters. *PRINT THE LETTER OF THE CORRECT ANSWER IN THE SPACE AT THE RIGHT.*

1. The EXTANT copies of the document were found in the safe.   1._____

   A. existing   B. original   C. forged   D. duplicate   E. torn

2. The recruit was more COMPLAISANT after the captain spoke to him.   2._____

   A. calm   B. affable   C. irritable   D. confident   E. arrogant

3. The man was captured under highly CREDITABLE circumstances.   3._____

   A. doubtful   B. believable   C. praiseworthy
   D. unexpected   E. unbelievable

4. The new employee appeared DIFFIDENT.   4._____

   A. contrary   B. haughty   C. conceited   D. unsure   E. confident

5. His superior officers were more SAGACIOUS than he.   5._____

   A. upset   B. obtuse   C. absurd   D. verbose   E. shrewd

_____

KEY (CORRECT ANSWERS)

1. A
2. B
3. C
4. D
5. E

_____

WORD MEANING
EXAMINATION SECTION

DIRECTIONS FOR THIS SECTION:
  For the following questions, select the word or group of words lettered A, B, C, D, or E that means MOST NEARLY the same as the word in capital letters. *PRINT THE LETTER OF THE CORRECT ANSWER IN THE SPACE AT THE RIGHT.*

TEST 1

1. To IMPLY means *most nearly* to
    A. agree to B. hint at C. laugh at D. mimic E. reduce   1. ...
2. APPRAISAL means *most nearly*
    A. allowance B. composition C. prohibition D. quantity E. valuation   2. ...
3. To DISBURSE means *most nearly* to
    A. approve B. expend C. prevent D. relay E. restrict   3. ...
4. POSTERITY means *most nearly*
    A. back payment   B. current procedure   C. final effort   4. ...
    D. future generations E. rare specimen
5. PUNCTUAL means *most nearly*
    A. clear B. honest C. polite D. prompt E. prudent   5. ...
6. PRECARIOUS means *most nearly*
    A. abundant B. alarmed C. cautious D. insecure E. placid   6. ...
7. To FOSTER means *most nearly* to
    A. delegate B. demote C. encourage D. plead E. surround   7. ...
8. PINNACLE means *most nearly*
    A. center B. crisis C. outcome D. peak E. personification   8. ...
9. COMPONENT means *most nearly*
    A. flattery B. opposite C. trend D. revision E. element   9. ...
10. To SOLICIT means *most nearly* to
    A. ask B. prohibit C. promise D. revoke E. surprise   10. ...
11. LIAISON means *most nearly*
    A. asset B. coordination C. difference D. policy E. procedure   11. ...
12. To ALLEGE means *most nearly* to
    A. assert B. break C. irritate D. reduce E. wait   12. ...
13. INFILTRATION means *most nearly*
    A. consumption B. disposal C. enforcement D. penetration E. seizure   13. ...
14. To SALVAGE means *most nearly* to
    A. announce B. combine C. prolong D. try E. save   14. ...
15. MOTIVE means *most nearly*
    A. attack B. favor C. incentive D. patience E. tribute   15. ...
16. To PROVOKE means *most nearly* to
    A. adjust B. incite C. leave D. obtain E. practice   16. ...
17. To SURGE means *most nearly* to
    A. branch B. contract C. revenge D. rush E. want   17. ...
18. To MAGNIFY means *most nearly* to
    A. attract B. demand C. generate D. increase E. puzzle   18. ...
19. PREPONDERANCE means *most nearly*
    A. decision B. judgment C. superiority D. submission E. warning   19. ...
20. To ABATE means *most nearly* to
    A. assist B. coerce C. diminish D. indulge E. trade   20. ...

TEST 2

1. AVARICE means *most nearly*
    A. flight B. greed C. pride D. thrift E. average   1. ...
2. PREDATORY means *most nearly*
    A. offensive B. plundering C. previous D. timeless E. perilous   2. ...

1

3. To VINDICATE means *most nearly* to   3. ...
   A. clear B. conquer C. correct D. illustrate E. alleviate
4. INVETERATE means *most nearly*   4. ...
   A. backward B. erect C. habitual D. lucky E. gradual
5. To DISCERN means *most nearly* to   5. ...
   A. describe B. fabricate C. recognize D. seek E. dilute
6. COMPLACENT means *most nearly*   6. ...
   A. indulgent B. listless C. overjoyed D. satisfied E. pliant
7. ILLICIT means *most nearly*   7. ...
   A. insecure B. unclear C. eligible D. unlimited E. unlawful
8. To PROCRASTINATE means *most nearly* to   8. ...
   A. declare B. multiply C. postpone D. steal E. proclaim
9. IMPASSIVE means *most nearly*   9. ...
   A. calm B. frustrated C. thoughtful D. unhappy E. perturbed
10. AMICABLE means *most nearly*   10. ...
    A. cheerful B. flexible C. friendly D. poised E. amorous
11. FEASIBLE means *most nearly*   11. ...
    A. breakable B. easy C. likeable D. practicable E. fearful
12. INNOCUOUS means *most nearly*   12. ...
    A. harmless B. insecure C. insincere D. unfavorable E. innate
13. OSTENSIBLE means *most nearly*   13. ...
    A. apparent B. hesitant C. reluctant D. showy E. concealed
14. INDOMITABLE means *most nearly*   14. ...
    A. excessive   B. unconquerable   C. unreasonable
    D. unthinkable   E. indubitable
15. CRAVEN means *most nearly*   15. ...
    A. carefree B. hidden C. miserly D. needed E. cowardly
16. To ALLAY means *most nearly* to   16. ...
    A. discuss B. quiet C. refine D. remove E. arrange
17. To ALLUDE means *most nearly* to   17. ...
    A. denounce B. refer C. state D. support E. align
18. NEGLIGENCE means *most nearly*   18. ...
    A. carelessness B. denial C. objection D. refusal E. eagerness
19. To AMEND means *most nearly* to   19. ...
    A. correct B. destroy C. end D. list E. dissent
20. RELEVANT means *most nearly*   20. ...
    A. conclusive B. careful C. obvious D. related E. incompetent

TEST 3

1. CONFIRM means *most nearly*   1. ...
   A. belong B. limit C. think over D. verify E. refine
2. PERILOUS means *most nearly*   2. ...
   A. dangerous B. mysterious C. tiring D. undesirable E. fickle
3. PROFICIENT means *most nearly*   3. ...
   A. likable B. obedient C. profitable D. profound E. skilled
4. IMPLICATE means *most nearly*   4. ...
   A. arrest B. confess C. involve D. question E. imply
5. ASSERT means *most nearly*   5. ...
   A. confide B. help C. state D. wish E. confirm
6. TEDIOUS means *most nearly*   6. ...
   A. boring B. easy C. educational D. difficult E. timorous
7. CONSEQUENCE means *most nearly*   7. ...
   A. punishment B. reason C. result D. tragedy E. basis
8. REPUTABLE means *most nearly*   8. ...
   A. durable B. effective C. powerful D. honorable E. tangible

2

9. REPROACH means *most nearly*
    A. anger B. blame C. pardon D. trap E. repel

                              9. ...

10. DIVERSE means *most nearly*
    A. confused B. indistinct C. unacceptable D. destructive E. unlike

                              10. ...

11. EVENTUAL means *most nearly*
    A. complete B. exciting C. final D. important E. enticing

                              11. ...

12. ACCESSORY means *most nearly*
    A. accomplice B. dishonest C. fugitive D. planner E. perpetrator

                              12. ...

13. ALLEVIATE means *most nearly*
    A. enrage B. increase C. lessen D. omit E. lift up

                              13. ...

14. RETICENT means *most nearly*
    A. doubtful B. humorous C. intelligent D. reserved E. reliant

                              14. ...

15. DILEMMA means *most nearly*
    A. caution B. decision C. hope D. direction E. predicament

                              15. ...

16. FLAUNT means *most nearly*
    A. compliment B. display C. punish D. warn E. reserve

                              16. ...

17. CONCUR means *most nearly*
    A. agree B. capture C. rescue D. trust E. disagree

                              17. ...

18. REPUDIATE means *most nearly*
    A. plot B. reject C. revise D. strike E. attest

                              18. ...

19. FRANTIC means *most nearly*
    A. criminal B. desperate C. jealous D. indirect E. sanguine

                              19. ...

20. PREMONITION means *most nearly*
    A. certainty B. forewarning C. puzzle D. thinking E. promise

                              20. ...

TEST 4

1. To CONTEND means *most nearly* to
    A. claim B. defeat C. refuse D. penalize E. contest

                              1. ...

2. EXPEDIENT means *most nearly*
    A. fearless B. suitable C. dishonest C. convincing E. famous

                              2. ...

3. PROPONENT means *most nearly*
    A. basic truth   B. witness   C. driver
    D. supporter   E. antongist

                              3. ...

4. DUBIOUS means *most nearly*
    A. uneventful B. silly C. uncertain D. untrue E. firm

                              4. ...

5. CONTRITE means *most nearly*
    A. painful B. sorry C. guilty D. hopeful E. joyful

                              5. ...

6. To CONCEDE means *most nearly* to
    A. suggest B. decide C. admit D. trust E. consign

                              6. ...

7. EQUITABLE means *most nearly*
    A. peaceful B. insurable C. lenient D. just E. equine

                              7. ...

8. To ALIGN means *most nearly* to
    A. cheat B. slander C. misinform D. criticize E. malinger

                              8. ...

9. To REPRIMAND means *most nearly* to
    A. shout B. scold C. complain D. punish E. recommend

                              9. ...

10. INFLEXIBLE means *most nearly*
    A. powerful B. impartial C. unpopular D. unbending E. lax

                              10. ...

11. INTACT means *most nearly*
    A. considerate B. inside C. whole D. lasting E. incomplete

                              11. ...

12. To DETER means *most nearly* to
    A. strike B. prevent C. disagree D. loosen E. detract

                              12. ...

13. PRUDENT means *most nearly*
    A. prudish B. strict C. stingy D. shy E. cautious

                              13. ...

14. REMISS MEANS *most nearly*
    A. neglectful B. dishonest C. prevented D. evil E. deceived

                              14. ...

15. APPREHENSIVE means *most nearly*
    A. dangerous B. harmful C. sad D. fearful E. approved

    15. ...

16. CONTRABAND means *most nearly*
    A. dissolved B. illegal C. fake D. unknown E. grouped

    16. ...

17. To DISSEMINATE means *most nearly* to
    A. spread B. mislead C. undermine D. disagree E. divert

    17. ...

18. CONTEMPT means *most nearly*
    A. pity B. hatred C. scorn D. brutality E. opinion

    18. ...

19. To HARASS means *most nearly* to
    A. retreat B. whip C. control D. torment E. harangue

    19. ...

20. OPAQUE means *most nearly*
    A. thick B. invisible C. lucid
    D. light colored E. not transparent

    20. ...

KEYS (CORRECT ANSWERS)

TEST 1	TEST 2	TEST 3	TEST 4
1. B	1. B	1. D	1. A
2. E	2. B	2. A	2. B
3. B	3. A	3. E	3. D
4. D	4. C	4. C	4. C
5. D	5. C	5. C	5. B
6. D	6. D	6. A	6. C
7. C	7. E	7. C	7. D
8. D	8. C	8. D	8. B
9. E	9. A	9. B	9. B
10. A	10. C	10. E	10. D
11. B	11. D	11. C	11. C
12. A	12. A	12. A	12. B
13. D	13. A	13. C	13. E
14. E	14. B	14. D	14. A
15. C	15. E	15. E	15. D
16. B	16. B	16. B	16. B
17. D	17. B	17. A	17. A
18. D	18. A	18. B	18. C
19. C	19. A	19. B	19. D
20. C	20. D	20. B	20. E

4

READING COMPREHENSION

UNDERSTANDING AND INTERPRETING
WRITTEN MATERIAL

TEST 1

DIRECTIONS FOR THIS SECTION:
   All questions are to be answered *SOLELY* on the basis of the information contained in the passage.
   Each question or incomplete statement is followed by several suggested answers or completions. Select the one that *BEST* answers the question or completes the statement. *PRINT THE LETTER OF THE CORRECT ANSWER IN THE SPACE AT THE RIGHT.*

Questions 1-7.

   Snow-covered roads spell trouble for motorists all winter long. Clearing highways of snow and ice to keep millions of motor vehicles moving freely is a tremendous task. Highway departments now rely, to a great extent, on chemical de-icers to get the big job done. Sodium chloride, in the form of commercial salt, is the de-icer most frequently used.
   There is no reliable evidence to prove that salt reduces highway accidents. But available statistics are impressive. For example, before Massachusetts used chemical de-icers, it had a yearly average of 21 fatal accidents and 1,635 injuries attributed to cars skidding on snow or ice. Beginning in 1990, the state began fighting hazardous driving *conditions with* chemical de-icers. During the period 1990-2000, there was a yearly average of only seven deaths and 736 injuries as a result of skids.
   Economical and effective in a moderately low temperature range, salt is increasingly popular with highway departments, but not so popular with individual car owners. Salty slush eats away at metal, including auto bodies. It also sprinkles windshields with a fine-grained spray which dries on contact, severely reducing visibility. However, drivers who are hindered or immobilized by heavy winter weather favor the liberal use of products such as sodium chloride. When snow blankets roads, these drivers feel that the quickest way to get back to the safety of driving on bare pavement is through use of de-icing salts.

   1. The *MAIN* reason given by the above passage for the use of sodium   1._____
      chloride as a de-icer is that it
      A. has no harmful side effects
      B. is economical
      C. is popular among car owners
      D. reduces highway accidents

2. The above passage may *BEST* be described as a(n)   2._____
   A. argument against the use of sodium chloride as a de-icer
   B. discussion of some advantages and disadvantages of sodium
      chloride as a de-icer
   C. recommendation to use sodium chloride as a de-icer
   D. technical account of the uses and effects of sodium chloride as a
      de-icer

3. Based on the above passage, the use of salt on snow-covered roadways   3._____
   will eventually
   A. decrease the efficiency of the automobile fuel
   B. cause tires to deteriorate
   C. damage the surface of the roadway
   D. cause holes in the sides of cars

4. The average number of persons killed yearly in Massachusetts in car   4._____
   accidents caused by skidding on snow or ice, before chemical de-icers
   were used there, was
   A. 9   B. 12   C. 21   D. 30

5. According to the passage, it would be advisable to use salt as a de-icer 5._____
   when
   A. outdoor temperatures are somewhat below freezing
   B. residues on highway surfaces are deemed to be undesirable
   C. snow and ice have low absorbency characteristics
   D. the use of a substance is desired which dries on contact

6. As a result of using chemical de-icers, the number of injuries resulting from 6._____
   skids in Massachusetts was reduced by about
   A. 35%   B. 45%   C. 55%   D. 65%

7. According to the above passage, driver visibility can be severely reduced 7._____
   by
   A. sodium chloride deposits on the windshield
   B. glare from salt and snow crystals
   C. salt spray covering the front lights
   D. faulty windshield wipers

Questions 8-10.

An employee should call the Fire Department for any fire except a small one in a
wastebasket. This kind of fire can be put out with a fire extinguisher. If the employee is
not sure about the size of the fire, he should not wait to find out how big it is. He should
call the Fire Department at once.

Every employee should know what to do when a fire starts. He should know how to
use the fire-fighting tools in the building and how to call the Fire Department. He should
also know where the nearest fire alarm box is. But the most important thing for an
employee to do in case of fire is to avoid panic.

8. If there is a small fire in a wastebasket, an employee should   8._____
    A. call the Fire Department
    B. let it burn itself out
    C. open a window
    D. put it out with a fire extinguisher

9. In case of fire, the most important thing for an employee to do is to   9._____
    A. find out how big it is
    B. keep calm
    C. leave the building right away
    D. report to his boss

10. If a large fire starts while he is at work, an employee should *always FIRST*   10._____
    A. call the Fire Department
    B. notify the Housing Superintendent
    C. remove inflammables from the building
    D. use a fire extinguisher

Questions 11-12.

Those correction theorists who are in agreement with severe and rigid controls as a normal part of the correctional process are confronted with a contradiction; this is so because a responsibility which is consistent with freedom cannot be developed in a repressive atmosphere. They do not recognize this contradiction when they carry out their programs with dictatorial force and expect convicted criminals exposed to such programs to be reformed into free and responsible citizens.

11. According to the above paragraph, those correction theorists are faced with   11._____
a contradiction who
    A. are in favor of the enforcement of strict controls in a prison
    B. believe that to develop a sense of responsibility, freedom must not
       be restricted
    C. take the position that the development of responsibility consistent
       with freedom is not possible in a repressive atmosphere
    D. think that freedom and responsibility can be developed only in a
       democratic atmosphere

12. According to the above paragraph, a repressive atmosphere in a prison   12._____
    A. does not conform to present-day ideas of freedom of the individual
    B. is admitted by correction theorists to be in conflict with the basic
       principles of the normal correctional process
    C. is advocated as the best method of maintaining discipline when
       rehabilitation is of secondary importance
    D. is not suitable for the development of a sense of responsibility
       consistent with freedom

Questions 13-16.

Abandoned cars – with tires gone, chrome stripped away, and windows smashed – have become a common sight on the City's streets. In 1990, more than 72,000 were deposited at curbs by owners who never came back, an increase of 15,000 from the year before and more than 30 times the number abandoned a decade ago. In January, 1991, the City's Environmental Protection Administrator asked the State Legislature to pass a law requiring a buyer of a new automobile to deposit $100 and an owner of an automobile at the time the law takes effect to deposit $50 with the State Department of Motor Vehicles. In return, they would be given a certificate of deposit which would be passed on to each succeeding owner. The final owner would get the deposit money back if he could present proof that he has disposed of his car "in an environmentally acceptable manner." The Legislature has given no indication that it plans to rush ahead on the matter.

13. The number of cars abandoned in City streets in 1980 was, most nearly,   13._____
    A. 2,500   B. 12,000   C. 27,500   D. 57,000

14. The proposed law would require a person who owned a car bought before   14._____
the law was passed to deposit
    A. $100 with the State Department of Motor Vehicles
    B. $50 with the Environmental Protection Administration
    C. $100 with the State Legislature
    D. $50 with the State Department of Motor Vehicles

15. The proposed law would require the State to return the deposit money *only*   15._____
when the
    A. original owner of the car shows proof that he sold it
    B. last owner of the car shows proof that he got rid of the car in a
       satisfactory way
    C. owner of the car shows proof that he has transferred the certificate
       of deposit to the next owner
    D. last owner of a car returns the certificate of deposit

16. The *main* idea or theme of the above article is that   16._____
    A. a proposed new law would make it necessary for car owners in the
       State to pay additional taxes
    B. the State Legislature is against a proposed law to require deposits
       from automobile owners to prevent them from abandoning their cars
    C. the City is trying to find a solution for the increasing number of cars
       abandoned on its streets
    D. to pay for the removal of abandoned cars, the City's Environmental
       Protection Administrator has asked the State to fine automobile
       owners who abandon their vehicles

Questions 17-19.

The German roach is the most common roach in houses in the United States. Adults are pale brown and about 1/2-inch long; both sexes have wings as long as the body, and can be distinguished from other roaches by the two dark stripes on the pronotum. The female carries its egg capsule protruding from her abdomen until the eggs are ready to hatch. This is the only common house-infesting species which carries the egg capsule for such an extended period of time. A female will usually produce 4 to 8 capsules in her lifetime. Each capsule contains 30 to 48 eggs which hatch out in about 28 days at ordinary room temperature. The completion of the nymphal stage under room conditions requires 40 to 125 days. German roaches may live as adults for as long as 303 days.

It is stated about that the German cockroach is the most commonly encountered of the house-infesting species in the United States. The reasons for this are somewhat complex, but the understanding of some of the factors involved are basic to the practice of pest control. In the first place, the German cockroach has a larger number of eggs per capsule and a shorter hatching time than do the other species. It also requires a shorter period from hatching until sexual maturity, so that within a given period of time a population of German roaches will produce a larger number of eggs. On the basis of this fact, we can state that this species has a high reproductive potential. Since the female carries the egg capsule during nearly the entire time that the embryos are developing within the egg, many hazards of the environment which may affect the eggs are avoided. This means that more nymphs are likely to hatch and that a larger portion of the reproductive potential is realized. The nymphs which hatch from each egg capsule tend to stay close to each other, and since they are often close to the female at time of hatching, there is a tendency for the population density to be high locally. Being smaller than most of the other roaches, they are able to conceal themselves in many places which are inaccessible to individuals of the larger species. All of these factors combined help to give the German cockroach an advantage with regard to group survival.

17. According to the above passage, the *most important* feature of the German roach which gives it an advantage over other roaches is its   17._____
    A. distinctive markings   B. immunity to disease
    C. long life span   D. power to reproduce

18. An *important* difference between an adult female German roach and an adult female of other species is the   18._____
    A. black bars or stripes which appear on the abdomen of the German roach
    B. German roach's preference for warm, moist places in which to breed
    C. long period of time during which the German roach carries the egg capsule
    D. presence of longer wings on the female German roach

19. A storeroom in a certain housing project has an infestation of German roaches, which includes 125 adult female. If the infestation is not treated and ordinary room temperature is maintained in the storeroom, *how many* eggs will hatch out during the lifetime of these females if they each lay 8 capsules containing 48 eggs each?   19._____
    A. 1,500   B. 48,000   C. 96,000   D. 303,000

Questions 20-22.

City governments have long had building codes which set minimum standards for building and for human occupancy. The code (or series of codes) makes provisions for standards of lighting and ventilation, sanitation, fire prevention, and protection. As a result of demands from manufacturers, builders, real estate people, tenement owners, and building-trades unions, these codes often have established minimum standards well below those that the contemporary society would accept as a rock-bottom minimum. Codes often become outdated, so that meager standards in one era become seriously inadequate a few decades later as society's concept of a minimum standard of living changes. Out-of-date codes, when still in use, have sometimes prevented the introduction of new devices and modern building techniques. Thus, it is extremely important that building codes keep pace with changes in the accepted concept of a minimum standard of living.

20. According to the above passage, all of the following considerations in building planning would probably be covered in a building code *EXCEPT*
    A. closet space as a percentage of total floor area
    B. size and number of windows required for rooms of differing sizes
    C. placement of fire escapes in each line of apartments
    D. type of garbage disposal units to be installed

20._____

21. According to the above passage, if an ideal building code were to be created, how would the established minimum standards in it compare to the ones that are presently set by city governments? They would
    A. *be lower* than they are at present
    B. *be higher* than they are at present
    C. *be comparable* to the present minimum standards
    D. *vary* according to the economic group that sets them

21._____

22. On the basis of the above passage, *what* is the reason for difficulties in introducing new building techniques?
    A. Builders prefer techniques which represent the rock-bottom minimum desired by society.
    B. Certain manufacturers have obtained patents on various building methods to the exclusion of new techniques.
    C. The government does not want to invest money in techniques that will soon be outdated.
    D. New techniques are not provided for in building codes which are not up to date.

22._____

Questions 23-25.

A flameproof fabric is defined as one which, when exposed to small sources of ignition such as sparks or smoldering cigarettes, does not burn beyond the vicinity of the source of the ignition. Cotton fabrics are the materials commonly used that are considered most hazardous. Other materials, such as acetate rayons and linens, are somewhat less hazardous, and woolens and some natural silk fabrics, even when untreated, are about the equal of the average treated cotton fabric insofar as flame spread and ease of ignition are concerned. The method of application is to immerse the fabric in a flameproofing solution. The container used must be large enough so that all the fabric is thoroughly wet and there are no folds which the solution does not penetrate.

23. According to the above paragraph, a flameproof fabric is one which   23._____
    A. is unaffected by heat and smoke
    B. resists the spread of flames when ignited
    C. burns with a cold flame
    D. cannot be ignited by sparks or cigarettes
    E. may smolder but cannot burn

24. According to the above paragraph, woolen fabrics which have not been   24._____
    flameproofed are as likely to catch fire as
    A. treated silk fabrics
    B. treated acetate rayon fabrics
    C. untreated linen fabrics
    D. untreated synthetic fabrics
    E. treated cotton fabrics

25. In the method described above, the flameproofing solution is *BEST* applied   25._____
    to the fabric by
    A. sponging the fabric   B. spraying the fabric
    C. dipping the fabric   D. brushing the fabric
    E. sprinkling the fabric

KEY (CORRECT ANSWERS)

1.	B	11.	A
2.	B	12.	D
3.	D	13.	A
4.	C	14.	D
5.	A	15.	B
6.	C	16.	C
7.	A	17.	D
8.	D	18.	C
9.	B	19.	B
10.	A	20.	A

21.	B
22.	D
23.	B
24.	E
25.	C

TEST 2

All questions are to be answered *SOLELY* on the basis of the information contained in the passage.

Each question or incomplete statement is followed by several suggested answers or completions. Select the one that *BEST* answers the question or completes the statement. *PRINT THE LETTER OF THE CORRECT ANSWER IN THE SPACE AT THE RIGHT.*

Questions 1-4.

Safety belts provide protection for the passengers of a vehicle by preventing them from crashing around inside if the vehicle is involved in a collision. They operate on the principle similar to that used in the packaging of fragile items. You become a part of the vehicle package and you are kept from being tossed about inside if the vehicle is suddenly decelerated. Many injury-causing collisions at low speeds – for example, at city intersections – could have been injury-free if the occupants had fastened their safety belts. There is a double advantage to the driver in that it not only protects him from harm, but prevents him from being yanked away from the wheel, thereby permitting him to maintain control of the car. Since, without seat belts, the risk of injury is about 50% greater, and the risk of death is about 30% greater, the State Vehicle and Traffic Law provided that a motor vehicle manufactured or assembled after June 30, 1964 and designated as a 1965 or later model should have two safety belts for the front seat. It also provides that a motor vehicle manufactured after June 30, 1966 and designated as a 1967 or later model should have at least one safety belt for the rear seat for each passenger for which the rear seat of such vehicle was designed.

1. The principle on which seat belts work is that
   A. a car and its driver and passengers are fragile
   B. a person fastened to the car will not be thrown around when the car slows down suddenly
   C. the driver and passengers of a car that is suddenly decelerated will be thrown forward
   D. the driver and passengers of an automobile should be packaged the way fragile items are packaged

1._____

2. We can assume from the above passage that safety belts should be worn at all times because you can never tell when
   A. a car will be forced to turn off onto another road
   B. it will be necessary to shift into low gear to go up a hill
   C. you will have to speed up to pass another car
   D. a car may have to come to a sudden stop

2._____

3. Besides preventing injury, an *additional* benefit from the use of safety belts is that
   A. collisions are fewer
   B. damage to the car is kept down
   C. the car can be kept under control
   D. the number of accidents at city intersections is reduced

3._____

4. The risk of death in car accidents for people who don't use safety belts is
   A. 30% greater than the risk of injury
   B. 30% greater than for those who do use them
   C. 50% less than the risk of injury
   D. 50% greater than for those who use them

4._____

Questions 5-9.

Any person who is living in New York City and is otherwise eligible may be granted public assistance whether or not he has New York State residence. However, since New York City does not contribute to the cost of assistance granted to persons who are without State residence, the cases of all recipients must be formally identified as to whether or not each member of the household has State residence.

To acquire State residence a person must have resided in New York State continuously for one year. Such residence is not lost unless the person is out of the State continuously for a period of one year or longer. Continuous residence does not include any period during which the individual is a patient in a hospital, an inmate of a public institution or of an incorporated private institution, a resident on a military reservation, or a minor residing in a boarding home while under the care of an authorized agency. Receipt of public assistance does not prevent a person from acquiring State residence. State residence, once acquired, is not lost because of absence from the State while a person is serving in the U. S. Armed Forces or the Merchant Marine; nor does a member of the family of such a person lose State residence while living with or near that person in these circumstances.

Each person, regardless of age, acquires or loses State residence as an individual. There is no derivative State residence except for an infant at the time of birth. He is deemed to have State residence if he is in the custody of both parents and either one of them has State residence, or if the parent having custody of him has State residence.

5. According to the above passage, an infant is deemed to have New York State residence at the time of his birth if
   A. he is born in New York State but neither of his parents is a resident
   B. he is in the custody of only one parent, who is not a resident, but his other parent is a resident
   C. his brother and sister are residents
   D. he is in the custody of both his parents but only one of them is a resident

5._____

6. The Jones family consists of five members. Jack and Mary Jones have lived in New York State continuously for the past eighteen months after having lived in Ohio since they were born. Of their three children, one was born ten months ago and has been in the custody of his parents since birth. Their second child lived in Ohio until six months ago and then moved in with his parents. Their third child had never lived in New York until he moved with his parents to New York eighteen months ago. However, he entered the armed forces one month later and has not lived in New York since that time.
   Based on the above passage, how many members of the Jones family are New York State residents?
   A. 2   B. 3   C. 4   D. 5

6._____

7.   Assuming that each of the following individuals has lived continuously in   7._____
New York State for the past year, and has never previously lived in the
State, *which one* of them is a New York State resident?
    A. Jack Salinas, who has been an inmate in a State correctional facility
for six months of the year
    B. Fran Johnson, who has lived on an Army base for the entire year
    C. Arlene Snyder, who married a non-resident during the past year
    D. Gary Phillips, who was a patient in a Veterans Administration
hospital for the entire year

8.   The above passage implies that the reason for determining whether or not   8._____
a recipient of public assistance is a State resident is that
    A. the cost of assistance for non-residents is not a New York City
responsibility
    B. non-residents living in New York City are not eligible for public
assistance
    C. recipients of public assistance are barred from acquiring State
residence
    D. New York City is responsible for the full cost of assistance to
recipients who are residents

9.   Assume that the Rollins household in New York City consists of six   9._____
members at the present time – Anne Rollins, her three children, her aunt,
and her uncle. Anne Rollins and one of her children moved to New York
City seven months ago. Neither of them had previously lived in New York
State. Her other two children have lived in New York City continuously for
the past two years, as has her aunt. Anne Rollins' uncle had lived in New
York City continuously for many years until two years ago. He then entered
the armed forces and has returned to New York City within the past month.
Based on the above passage, how many members of the Rollins'
household are New York State residents?
    A. 2   B. 3   C. 4   D. 6

Questions 10-12.

     The agreement under which a tenant rents property from a landlord is known as a
lease. Generally speaking, leases are classified as either short-term or long-term in
duration. They are further subdivided according to the method used to determine the
amount of periodic rent payments. Of the many types of lease in use, the more
commonly used ones are the following:

1. The straight or fixed lease is one in which rent may be paid in equal amounts
throughout the duration of the lease. These are usually restricted to short-term
leasing, or somewhat longer-term if clauses in the lease provide for periodic
escalation of payments as the economy shifts.
2. Percentage leasing, used for short-term commercial leasing, provides the landlord
with a stipulated percentage of a tenant's gross sales from goods and services sold
on the premises, in addition to a fixed amount of rent.
3. The net lease, generally long-term (ten years or more), requires the tenant to pay all
operating costs, including real estate taxes and insurance. In a net-net lease, the
tenant further agrees to meet mortgage interest and principal payments.

4. An escalated lease, which is a long-term lease, requires rent to be of a stipulated base amount which periodically is subject to escalation in accordance with cost-of-living index scales, or in direct proportion to taxes, insurance, and operating costs.

10. Based on the information given in the passage, *which* type of lease is *most likely* to be advantageous to a landlord if there is a high rate of inflation?   10._____
    A. fixed lease   B. percentage lease
    C. net lease   D. escalated lease

11. On the basis of the above passage, *which* types of lease would generally be *MOST* suitable for a well-established textile company which requires permanent facilities for its large operations?   11._____
    A. Percentage lease and escalated lease
    B. Escalated lease and net lease
    C. Straight lease and net lease
    D. Straight lease and percentage lease

12. According to the above passage, the *only* type of lease which assures the same amount of rent throughout a specified interval is the   12._____
    A. straight lease   B. percentage lease
    C. net-net lease   D. escalated lease

Questions 13-18.

Basic to every office is the need for proper lighting. Inadequate lighting is a familiar cause of fatigue and serves to create a somewhat dismal atmosphere in the office. One requirement of proper lighting is that it be of an appropriate intensity. Intensity is measured in foot-candles. According to the Illuminating Engineering Society of New York, for casual seeing tasks such as in reception rooms, inactive file rooms, and other service areas, it is recommended that the amount of light be 30 foot-candles. For ordinary seeing tasks such as reading and work in active file rooms and in mail rooms, the recommended lighting is 100 foot-candles. For very difficult seeing tasks such as accounting, transcribing, and business-machine use, the recommended lighting is 150 foot-candles.

Lighting intensity is only one requirement. Shadows and glare are to be avoided. For example, the larger the proportion of a ceiling filled with lighting units, the more glare-free and comfortable the lighting will be. Natural lighting from windows is not too dependable because on dark wintry days windows yield little usable light, and on sunny, summer afternoons the glare from windows may be very distracting. Desks should not face the windows. Finally, the main lighting source ought to be overhead and to the left of the user.

13. According to the above passage, insufficient light in the office may cause   13._____
    A. glare   B. shadows   C. tiredness   D. distraction

14. Based on the above passage, *which* of the following must be considered when planning lighting arrangements? The   14._____
    A. amount of natural light present
    B. amount of work to be done
    C. level of difficulty of work to be done
    D. type of activity to be carried out

15. It can be inferred from the above passage that a well-coordinated lighting   15._____
scheme is likely to result in
    A. greater employee productivity
    B. elimination of light reflection
    C. lower lighting cost
    D. more use of natural light

16. Of the following, the *BEST* title for the above passage is: 16._____
    A. Characteristics of Light
    B. Light Measurement Devices
    C. Factors to Consider When Planning Lighting Systems
    D. Comfort vs. Cost When Devising Lighting Arrangements

17. According to the above passage, a foot-candle is a measurement of the   17._____
    A. number of bulbs used
    B. strength of the light
    C. contrast between glare and shadow
    D. proportion of the ceiling filled with lighting units

18. According to the above passage, the number of foot-candles of light that   18._____
would be needed to copy figures onto a payroll is
    A. less than 30 foot-candles   B. 30 foot-candles
    C. 100 foot-candles   D. 150 foot-candles

Questions 19-22.

A summons is an official statement ordering a person to appear in court. In traffic violation situations, summonses are used when arrests need not be made. The main reason for traffic summonses is to deter motorists from repeating the same traffic violation. Occasionally, motorists may make unintentional driving errors and sometimes they are unaware of correct driving regulations. In cases such as these, the policy should be to have the Officer verbally inform the motorist of the violation and warn him against repeating it. The purpose of this practice is not to limit the number of summonses, but rather to prevent the issuing of summonses when the violation is not due to deliberate intent or to inexcusable negligence.

19. According to the above passage, the *PRINCIPAL* reason for issuing traffic   19._____
summonses is to
    A. discourage motorists from violating these laws again
    B. increase the money collected by the city
    C. put traffic violators in prison
    D. have them serve as substitutes for police officers

20. The reason a verbal warning may sometimes be substituted for a summons   20._____
is to
    A. limit the number of summonses
    B. distinguish between excusable and inexcusable violations
    C. provide harsher penalties for deliberate intent than for inexcusable
      negligence
    D. decrease the caseload in the courts

21. The author of the above passage feels that someone who violated a traffic   21._____
regulation because he did *not* know about the regulation should be
    A. put under arrest   B. fined less money
    C. given a summons   D. told not to do it again

22. Using the distinctions made by the author of the above passage, the *one* of   22._____
the following motorists to whom it would be *MOST* desirable to issue a
summons is the one who exceeded the speed limit because he
    A. did not know the speed limit
    B. was late for an important business appointment
    C. speeded to avoid being hit by another car
    D. had a speedometer which was not working properly

Questions 23-25.

       Physical design plays a very significant role in crime rate. Crime rate has been
found to increase almost proportionately with building height. The average number of
crimes is much greater in higher buildings than in lower ones (equal to or less than six
stories). What is most interesting is that in buildings of six stories or less, the project size
or total number of units does not make a difference. It seems that, although larger
projects encourage crime by fostering feelings of anonymity, isolation, irresponsibility,
and lack of identity with surroundings, evidence indicates that larger projects
encompassed in low buildings seem to offset what we may assume to be factors
conducive to high crime rates. High-rise projects not only experience a higher rate of
crime within the buildings, but a greater proportion of the crime occurs in the interior
public spaces of these buildings as compared with those of the lower buildings. Lower
buildings have more limited public space than higher ones. A criminal probably
perceives that the interior public areas of buildings are where his victims are most
vulnerable and where the possibility of his being seen or apprehended is minimal.
Placement of elevators, entrance lobbies, fire stairs and secondary exits all are factors
related to the likelihood of crimes taking place in buildings. The study of all of these
elements should bear some weight in the planning of new projects.

23. According to the passage, *which* of the following *BEST* describes the   23._____
relationship between building size and crime?
    A. Larger projects lead to a greater crime rate
    B. Higher buildings tend to increase the crime rate
    C. The smaller the number of project apartments in low buildings the
        higher the crime rate
    D. Anonymity and isolation serve to lower the crime rate in small
        buildings

24. According to the passage, the likelihood of a criminal attempting a mugging   24._____
in the interior public portions of a high-rise building is good because
    A. tenants will be constantly flowing in and out of the area
    B. there is easy access to fire stairs and secondary exits
    C. there is a good chance that no one will see him
    D. tenants may not recognize the victims of crime as their neighbors

25. *Which* of the following is *implied* by the passage as an explanation for the   25._____
fact that the crime rate is lower in large low-rise housing projects than in
large high-rise projects?
    A. Tenants know each other better and take a greater interest in what
       happens in the project
    B. There is more public space where tenants are likely to gather
       together
    C. The total number of units in a low-rise project is fewer than the total
       number of units in a high-rise project
    D. Elevators in low-rise buildings travel quickly, thus limiting the
       amount of time in which a criminal can act

KEY (CORRECT ANSWERS)

1.	B	11.	B
2.	D	12.	A
3.	C	13.	C
4.	B	14.	D
5.	D	15.	A
6.	B	16.	C
7.	C	17.	B
8.	A	18.	D
9.	C	19.	A
10.	D	20.	B

21.	D
22.	B
23.	B
24.	C
26.	A

READING COMPREHENSION
UNDERSTANDING AND INTERPRETING WRITTEN MATERIAL
EXAMINATION SECTION
TEST 1

DIRECTIONS: Each question or incomplete statement is followed by
several suggested answers or completions. Select the
one that BEST answers the question or completes the
statement. *PRINT THE LETTER OF THE CORRECT ANSWER IN
THE SPACE AT THE RIGHT.*

Questions 1-5.

DIRECTIONS: Questions 1 through 5 are based on the following passage.
You are to answer the questions which follow based SOLELY
upon the information in the passage.

More than 700 dolphins and whales piled up on France's Atlantic
coast last February and March. Most were common dolphins, but the
toll also included striped and bottlenose dolphins -- even a few
harbor porpoises and fin, beaked, pilot, and minke whales. Many
victims had ropes around their tails or had heads or tails cut off;
some had been partly butchered for food. To scientists the cause is
obvious: These marine mammals were seen as waste, *bycatch*, to the
fishermen who snared them in their nets while seeking commercial fish.

Mid-water trawlers are responsible for this, not drift nets, says
Anne Collet, a French biologist who examined the carcasses. The
European Union has banned large drift nets. Two other European
treaties call for bycatch reduction by vessels using huge trawls for
hake and other species. But the Bay of Biscay falls beyond the
treaties, a painfully obvious loophole.

1. What killed the dolphins and whales at the Bay of Biscay?   1.___
    A. The propellers of recreational motorboats
    B. Fishermen using drift nets to catch commercial fish
    C. Fishermen seeking commercial fish
    D. Fishermen seeking their tails and heads as trophies

2. What is *bycatch*?   2.___
    A. Animals accidentally caught in the same nets used to
       catch other types of fish
    B. Animals which typically gather close to certain types
       of fish, allowing fishermen to hunt more than one
       species at a time
    C. Those parts of animals and fish discarded by fisher-
       men after the catch
    D. Those fish which exceed the fisherman's specified
       limit and must be thrown back

3. The dolphins and whales were killed around the Bay of   3.___
    Biscay because the
    A. treaties which protect these species of dolphins and
       whales do not reach the Bay of Biscay
    B. bodies of the animals were dumped at the Bay of
       Biscay, but scientists do not know where they were
       killed

    C. treaties which limit the use of drift nets do not
       reach the Bay of Biscay
    D. treaties which limit the use of trawls do not reach
       the Bay of Biscay

4. Where is the Bay of Biscay located?   4.___
    A. France's Pacific coast
    B. France's Atlantic coast
    C. The European Union's Atlantic coast
    D. The French Riviera

5. What types of fish are mid-water trawlers usually used   5.___
   for?
    A. Common, striped, and bottlenose dolphins
    B. Common dolphins, harbor porpoises, and pilot whales
    C. Hake and pilot, minke, fin, and beaked whales
    D. Hake and other species

Questions 6-10.

DIRECTIONS: Questions 6 through 10 are based on the following
              passage. You are to answer the questions which follow
              based SOLELY upon the information in the passage.

Malaria once infected 9 out of 10 people in North Borneo, now
known as Brunei. In 1955, the World Health Organization (WHO) began
spraying the island with dieldrin (a DDT relative) to kill malaria-
carrying mosquitoes. The program was so successful that the dread
disease was virtually eliminated.

Other, unexpected things began to happen, however. The dieldrin
also killed other insects, including flies and cockroaches living in
houses. At first, the islanders applauded this turn of events, but
then small lizards that also lived in the houses died after gorging
themselves on dieldrin-contaminated insects. Next, cats began dying
after feeding on the lizards. Then, in the absence of cats, rats
flourished and overran the villages. Now that the people were
threatened by sylvatic plague carried by rat fleas, WHO parachuted
healthy cats onto the island to help control the rats.

Then the villagers' roofs began to fall in. The dieldrin had
killed wasps and other insects that fed on a type of caterpillar that
either avoided or was not affected by the insecticide. With most of
its predators eliminated, the caterpillar population exploded, munch-
ing its way through its favorite food: the leaves used in thatched
roofs.

Ultimately, this episode ended happily: Both malaria and the
unexpected effects of the spraying program were brought under control.
Nevertheless, the chain of unforeseen events emphasizes the unpredic-
tability of interfering in an ecosystem.

6. The World Health Organization (WHO) began spraying dieldrin   6.___
   on North Borneo in order to
      A. kill the bacteria which causes malaria
      B. kill the mosquitoes that carry malaria
      C. disrupt the foodchain so that malaria-carrying mos-
         quitoes would die
      D. kill the mosquitoes, flies, and cockroaches that carry
         malaria

7. Which of the following did the dieldrin kill?   7.___
      A. Mosquitoes   B. Rats
      C. Caterpillars   D. All of the above

8. The villagers' roofs caved in because the dieldrin killed   8.___
      A. mosquitoes, flies, rats, and cats
      B. the trees whose leaves are used in thatched roofs
      C. the caterpillar that eats the leaves used in thatched
         roofs
      D. the predators of the caterpillar that eats the leaves
         used in thatched roofs

9. Which of the following was NOT a side effect of spraying   9.___
   dieldrin on Borneo?
      A. Malaria was virtually eliminated.
      B. The rat population exploded.
      C. The cat population exploded.
      D. The caterpillar population exploded.

10. Why did the World Health Organization (WHO) deliver   10.___
    healthy cats to Borneo without trying to replenish the
    other animals and insects which had been wiped out by the
    dieldrin?
    The
      A. presence of a healthy cat population was all that was
         required to restore the balanced ecosystem
      B. rats that cats preyed upon carried an illness
         threatening to humans
      C. other insects and animals killed by the dieldrin were
         nuisances and the villagers were happy to be free of
         them
      D. villagers' had become attached to cats as domestic
         pets

Questions 11-15.

DIRECTIONS: Questions 11 through 15 are based on the following
              passage. You are to answer the questions which follow
              based SOLELY upon the information in the passage.

    Historically, towns and cities grew as a natural byproduct of
people choosing to live in certain areas for agricultural, business,
or recreational reasons. Beginning in the 1920s, private and
governmental planners began to think about how an ideal town would

be planned. These communities would be completely built before houses were offered for sale. This concept of preplanning, designing, and building an ideal town was not fully developed until the 1960s. By 1976, about forty-three towns could be classified as planned *new towns*.

One example of a new town is Reston, Virginia, located about 40 kilometers west of Washington, D.C. Reston began to accept residents in 1964 and has a projected population of eighty thousand. Because developers tried to preserve the great natural beauty of the area and the high quality of architectural design of its buildings, Reston has attracted much attention. Reston also has innovative programs in education, government, transportation, and recreation. For example, the stores in Reston are within easy walking distance of the residential parts of the community, and there are many open spaces for family activities. Because Reston is not dependent upon the automobile, noise and air pollution have been greatly reduced. Recent research indicates that the residents of Reston have rated their community much higher than residents of less well-planned suburbs.

11. When did the concept of first building a town and then offering houses for sale fully develop?   11.___
    A. 1920s   B. 1950s   C. 1960s   D. 1970s

12. The goal of planners who develop and build ideal towns and suburbs is to   12.___
    A. eliminate the tendency of towns and cities to naturally develop around business or recreational centers
    B. control population growth
    C. regulate the resources devoted to housing and recreation
    D. cut down on suburban sprawl by developing communities where residents are not dependent on cars to maintain a high quality of living

13. Which of the following goals did developers have in mind when planning the community of Reston?   13.___
      I. Preservation of natural beauty
     II. Communal living spaces
    III. Communal recreational spaces
     IV. High standards of architectural design

    The CORRECT answer is:
      A. I, II, III, IV   B. I, III, IV
      C. II, III, IV   D. I, II, IV

14. The fact that stores in Reston are within easy walking distance of the residential parts of the community is an example of innovation in   14.___
      A. transportation   B. recreation
      C. education   D. all of the above

15. What are the environmental advantages to towns like 15.___
    Reston?
    A. Uniform architecture
    B. Individual recreational spaces cut down on the
       overuse of resources
    C. Decreased noise and air pollution
    D. Ability to control the number and type of residents

Questions 16-20.

DIRECTIONS: Questions 16 through 20 are based on the following
            passage. You are to answer the questions which follow
            based SOLELY upon the information in the passage.

Lead is one of the most common toxic (harmful or poisonous)
metals in the intercity environment. It is found, to some extent,
in all parts of the urban environment (e.g., air, soil, and older
pipes and paint) and in all biological systems, including people.
There is no apparent biologic need for lead, but it is sufficiently
concentrated in the blood and bones of children living in inner cities
to cause health and behavior problems. In some populations over 20%
of the children have levels of lead concentrated in their blood above
that believed safe. Lead affects nearly every system of the body.
Acute lead toxicity may be characterized by a variety of symptoms,
including anemia, mental retardation, palsy, coma, seizures, apathy,
uncoordination, subtle loss of recently acquired skills, and bizarre
behavior. Lead toxicity is particularly a problem for young children
who tend to be exposed to higher concentrations in some urban areas
and apparently are more susceptible to lead poisoning than are adults.
Following exposure to lead and having acute toxic response, some
children manifest aggressive, difficult to manage behavior.

The occurrence of lead toxicity or lead poisoning has cultural,
political, and sociological implications. Over 2,000 years ago, the
Roman Empire produced and used tremendous amounts of lead for a
period of several hundred years. Production rates were as high as
55,000 metric tons per year. Romans had a wide variety of uses for
lead, including pots in which grapes were crushed and processed into
a syrup for making wine, cups, and goblets from which the wine was
drunk, as a base for cosmetics and medicines, and finally for the
wealthy class of people who had running water in their homes, lead
was used to make the pipes that carried the water. It has been
argued by some historians that gradual lead poisoning among the
upper class in Rome was partly responsible for Rome's eventual fall.

16. In which parts of the urban environment can lead be found? 16.___
    I. Air   II. Water
    III. Adults   IV. Children

    The CORRECT answer is:
    A. I, II, III   B. I, III, IV
    C. II, III, IV   D. All of the above

17. Lead toxicity has the most powerful effect on which of   17.___
    the following?
    A. Mentally retarded children
    B. Young children
    C. Anemic women
    D. Children who suffer from seizures

18. Romans used lead in which of the following?   18.___
    A. Cosmetics B. Paint   C. Wine   D. Clothes

19. Humans require a certain level of lead in the bloodstream   19.___
    in order to avoid which of the following?
    A. Anemia
    B. Uncoordination
    C. Seizures
    D. Scientists have found no biological need for lead
       among humans

20. Which of the following would most directly support the   20.___
    theory that lead poisoning was partially responsible for
    the fall of Rome?
    A. Evidence of bizarre behavior among ancient Roman
       leaders
    B. Evidence of lead in the drinking water of ancient
       Rome
    C. Studies analyzing the lead content of bones of ancient
       Romans which detect increased levels of lead
    D. Evidence of lead in the environment of ancient Rome

Questions 21-25.

DIRECTIONS: Questions 21 through 25 are based on the following
             passage. You are to answer the questions which follow
             based SOLELY upon the information in the passage.

The city of Venice, Italy has been known to be slowly sinking,
but for a long time no one knew the cause or a solution. Floods
were becoming more and more common, especially during the winter
storms when the winds drove waters from the Adriatic Sea into the
city's streets. Famous for its canals and architectural beauty,
Venice was in danger of being destroyed by the very lagoon that had
sustained its commerce for more than a thousand years. Then the
reason that the city was sinking was discovered: groundwater in the
region was being pumped out and used; the depletion of the water
table, over time, caused the soil to compress under the weight of
the city above it. The wells that influenced Venice, which were
located on the Italian mainland as well as on the islands that make
up Venice, supplied water to nearly industrial and domestic users.

Once the cause was discovered, the wells were capped and other
sources of water were found; as a result the city has stopped sinking.
This is an example of the application of scientific research on the
environment to achieve a solution helpful to a major city.

21. What causes the winter floods in Venice?
    A. The disintegration of the canals that used to protect the city from the floods
    B. Storms that drive waters from the wells into the streets
    C. The flawed canal system for which the city is famous
    D. Storms that drive waters from the Adriatic Sea into the streets

21.___

22. Venice was sinking because of depletion of the
    A. lagoon upon which the city was founded
    B. wells used to flood the lagoons
    C. water table beneath the city
    D. soil beneath the city

22.___

23. What was the water beneath Venice used for?
    A. Wastewater
    B. To supply water to the famous canals
    C. To supply drinking water to Venetians
    D. To supply local industrial users

23.___

24. How was the problem remedied?
    A. City leaders regulated use of the wells and found other sources of water.
    B. The wells were capped.
    C. Flood water was diverted back to the Adriatic Sea.
    D. The wells were used to supply water to nearby industrial and domestic users.

24.___

25. How were scientists able to restore Venice to its proper (and previous) elevation?
    A. Venice was not restored to its previous elevation
    B. By diverting water back into the soil beneath Venice
    C. By capping the wells and finding other sources of water
    D. By restoring the water table

25.___

KEY (CORRECT ANSWERS)

1. C	6. B	11. C	16. D	21. D
2. A	7. A	12. D	17. B	22. C
3. D	8. D	13. B	18. A	23. D
4. B	9. C	14. A	19. D	24. B
5. D	10. B	15. C	20. C	25. A

TEST 2

DIRECTIONS: Each question or incomplete statement is followed by several suggested answers or completions. Select the one that BEST answers the question or completes the statement. *PRINT THE LETTER OF THE CORRECT ANSWER IN THE SPACE AT THE RIGHT*.

Questions 1-5.

DIRECTIONS: Questions 1 through 5 are based on the following passage. You are to answer the questions which follow based SOLELY upon the information in the passage.

China, with one-fifth of the world's population, is the most populous country in the world. Between 1980 and 1995, China's population grew by 200 million people -- about three-fourths of the population of the United States -- to reach 1.2 billion. Although its growth rate is expected to slow somewhat in the coming decades, population experts predict that there will be 1.5 billion Chinese by 2025. But can China's food production continue to keep pace with its growing population? Should China develop a food deficit, it may need to import more grain from other countries than those countries can spare from their own needs.

To give some idea of the potential impact of China on the world's food supply, consider the following examples. All of the grain produced by Norway would be needed to supply two more beers to each person in China. If the Chinese were to eat as much fish as the Japanese do, China would consume the entire world fish catch. Food for all the chickens required for China to reach its goal of 200 eggs per person per year by 2010 will equal all the grain exported by Canada -- the world's second largest grain exporter. Increased demand by China for world grain supplies could result in dramatic increases in food prices and precipitate famines in other areas of the world.

1. China's population increased between 1980 and 1995 by   1.___
   A. 200 million people
   B. 1.2 billion people
   C. 1.5 billion people
   D. one-fifth of the world's population

2. If China developed a food deficit, which of the following   2.___
   would most negatively affect the world's supply of food?
   A. Famines resulting from the increased price of grain
   B. Domestic increase in the production of grain to meet the needs of the Chinese people
   C. International increase in the production of grain to meet China's need
   D. Importing more grain from other countries than those countries could spare

3. Which of the following was a goal the Chinese government   3.___
   hoped to reach by 2010?
   A. Importing Canada's entire supply of grain
   B. Supplying 200 eggs annually to every citizen
   C. A population of 1.5 billion people
   D. Supplying enough fish to each citizen to match
      Japan's consumption

4. Which of the following countries exports the most grain?   4.___
   A. China   B. Norway   C. Canada   D. Japan

5. Which of the following groups contains 200 million people?   5.___
   A. The current population of the United States
   B. Three-quarters of the population of the United States
   C. China's current population
   D. Three-quarters of the population of China

Questions 6-10.

DIRECTIONS: Questions 6 through 10 are based on the following
              passage. You are to answer the questions which follow
              based SOLELY upon the information in the passage.

On Tuesday, 16 June 1987, the last dusky seaside sparrow (*Ammo-dramus maratimus nigrescens*) died in captivity at Walt Disney World's Discovery Island Zoological Park in Orlando, Florida. The bird was a male that was probably about twelve years old. Originally, this subspecies and several other subspecies were found in the coastal salt marshes on the Atlantic coast of Floria. (A subspecies is a distinct population of a species that has several characteristics that distinguish it from other populations.) One other subspecies, the Smyrna seaside sparrow (*Ammodramus maratimus pelonata*), is believed to have become extinct several years ago, and a third sub-species, the Cape Sable seaside sparrow (*Ammodramus maratimus mirabilis*), was listed as an endangered species in 1967. Before the deaths of the last remaining dusky seaside sparrows, a few males were crossed with another subspecies, Scott's seaside sparrow (*Ammodramus maratimus peninsulae*). Thus, the hybrid offspring between these two subspecies contain some of the genes that made the dusky seaside sparrow unique.

The endangerment and extinction of these different birds was a direct result of the land development and drainage that destroyed the salt-marsh habitat to which they were adapted. The development of Cape Canaveral as a major center for the U.S. space program also resulted in the modification of much of the birds' original habitat and was a partial cause of their extinction.

6. Which of the following subspecies is NOT yet extinct?   6.___
   A. Dusky seaside sparrow
   B. Cape Sable seaside sparrow
   C. Smyrna seaside sparrow
   D. All of the listed subspecies are extinct

7. A subspecies is a population   7.___
    A. within a species that has been crossed with another
       population within the same species in order to avoid
       extinction
    B. within a subspecies that has distinguishing character-
       istics
    C. that has distinguishing characteristics
    D. within a species that has distinguishing characteris-
       tics

8. What was the dusky seaside sparrow's natural habitat?   8.___
    A. Coastal salt marshes of Florida
    B. Man-made parks and zoos such as Discovery Land
    C. Flat, desert-like plains around Cape Canaveral
    D. Areas of land development

9. A hybrid is an animal that   9.___
    A. cannot reproduce
    B. is extinct
    C. is the result of a cross between two subspecies
    D. is the result of a cross between two species

10. What caused the extinction of the dusky seaside sparrow?   10.___
    A. An overabundance of predators caused by human influ-
       ence and development
    B. Destruction of its natural habitat by human develop-
       ment
    C. Inability to reproduce in captivity
    D. All of the above

Questions 11-15.

DIRECTIONS: Questions 11 through 15 are based on the following
                 passage. You are to answer the questions which follow
                 based SOLELY upon the information in the passage.

For more than 600 years only Adelie penguins lived along the
chilly shores of the Western Antarctic Peninsula in the Palmer region.
Ornithologist and paleontologist Steven Emslie of the University of
North Carolina, Wilmington, found Adelie bones in nests near Palmer
Station dating from as early as the 14th century.

But two other penguin species have moved in, apparently as the
result of a 50-year warming trend that has seen winter temperatures
rise seven to nine degrees F and lessened the amount of ice around
the peninsula. *Adelies require the edges of pack ice for foraging,*
Emslie says. As the ice shrinks, he believes, their numbers decline.
Chinstrap penguins, which forage in the open ocean and aren't affected
by ice breakup, began to arrive in the 1950s. Gentoos, normally a
subantarctic species, first appeared here in 1975. The two newcomers
now form a major portion of the region's penguin population.

11. When did new penguin species begin arriving in the Palmer   11.___
    region?
    A. 1400s   B. 1950s   C. 1975   D. 1990s

12. Which of the following penguin species are NOT affected   12.___
    by ice breakup?
    A. Adelie   B. Gentoos   C. Chinstrap   D. Emslie

13. What has caused the new penguin species to move into the   13.___
    Palmer region?
    A. A warming trend
    B. An increase in the amount of pack ice around the
       peninsula
    C. An increase in the availability of food
    D. All of the above

14. Adelie penguins have lived in the Palmer region since   14.___
    A. the 14th century   B. the early 1900s
    C. the 1950s   D. 1975

15. What effect does the decrease in the amount of pack ice   15.___
    have on Adelie penguins?
    A. Decreased ability to fight off predators
    B. Increased ability to fight off predators
    C. Increased ability to forage for food
    D. Decreased ability to forage for food

Questions 16-20.

DIRECTIONS: Questions 16 through 20 are based on the following
              passage. You are to answer the questions which follow
              based SOLELY upon the information in the passage.

     The price of a liter of gasoline is determined by two major
factors: (1) the cost of purchasing and processing crude oil into
gasoline, and (2) various taxes. Most of the differences in gasoline
prices between countries are a result of the differences in taxes and
reflect differences in government policy toward motor vehicle transportation.

     A major objective of governments is to collect money to build
and repair roads, and governments often charge the user by taxing the
fuel used by the car or truck. Governments can also discourage the
use of automobiles by increasing the cost of fuel. An increase in
fuel costs also creates a demand for increased fuel efficiency in
all forms of motor transport.

     Many European countries raise more money from fuel taxes than
they spend on building and repairing roads, while the United States
raises approximately 60 percent of the moneys needed for roads from
fuel taxes. The relatively low cost of fuel in the United States
encourages more travel and increases road repair costs. The cost of
taxes to the United States consumer is about 20 percent of the cost of
fuel, while in Japan and many European countries, the percentage is
60 to 75 percent.

16. Which of the following is likely to result from an
    increase in the cost of fuel?   16.___
    A. *Decreased* fuel efficiency
    B. *Increased* fuel efficiency
    C. *Increased* travel
    D. *Increased* road repair costs

17. Which of the following affects the price of gasoline?   17.___
    A. Cost of purchasing crude oil
    B. Cost of processing crude oil
    C. Taxes
    D. All of the above

18. Most governments tax car and truck fuel in order to   18.___
    A. finance the costs of repairing roads
    B. discourage motor travel as much as possible
    C. finance various social welfare programs
    D. finance public transportation systems

19. Differences in _____ accounts for the differences in   19.___
    gasoline prices between countries.
    A. the cost of purchasing a car
    B. the amount of crude oil each country exports
    C. government taxes
    D. the number of automobiles imported by individual
       countries

20. Which of the following is most likely to discourage   20.___
    travel?
    A. *Decrease* in fuel tax
    B. *Increase* in fuel tax
    C. *Decrease* in fuel efficiency
    D. *Increase* in road repair

Questions 21-25.

DIRECTIONS: Questions 21 through 25 are based on the following
             passage. You are to answer the questions which follow
             based SOLELY upon the information in the passage.

    Wyoming rancher Jack Turnell is one of a new breed of cowpuncher
who gets along with environmentalists. He talks about riparian ecology
and biodiversity as fluently as he talks about cattle. *I guess I have
learned how to bridge the gap between the environmentalists, the
bureaucracies, and the ranching industry.*

    Turnell grazes cattle on his 32,000-hectare (80,000 acre) ranch
south of Cody, Wyoming, and on 16,000 hectares (40,000 acres) of
Forest Service land on which he has grazing rights. For the first
decade after he took over the ranch, he punched cows the conventional
way. Since then, he's made some changes.

Turnell disagrees with the proposals by environmentalists to raise grazing fees and remove sheep and cattle from public rangeland. He believes that if ranchers are kicked off the public range, ranches like his will be sold to developers and chopped up into vacation sites, irreversibly destroying the range for wildlife and livestock alike.

At the same time, he believes that ranches can be operated in more ecologically sustainable ways. To demonstrate this, Turnell began systematically rotating his cows away from the riparian areas, gave up most uses of fertilizers and pesticides, and crossed his Hereford and Angus cows with a French breed that tends to congregate less around water. Most of his ranching decisions are made in consultation with range and wildlife scientists, and changes in range condition are carefully monitored with photographs.

The results have been impressive. Riparian areas on the ranch and Forest Service land are lined with willows and other plant life, providing lush habitat for an expanding population of wildlife, including pronghorn antelope, deer, moose, elk, bear, and mountain lions. And this *eco-rancher* now makes more money because the higher-quality grass puts more meat on his cattle. He frequently talks to other ranchers about sustainable range management; some of them probably think he has been chewing locoweed.

21. The fact that Turnell's decision-making process involves   21.___
    range and wildlife scientists is an example of
       A. successful government oversight
       B. enforced government regulation
       C. conventional ranching
       D. successful sustainable ranching

22. What is the environmental drawback to removing grazing   22.___
    animals from government range land?
       A. The loss of ranches which rely on public ranges to
          real-estate developers
       B. The loss of public range land to real-estate developers
       C. Under-use of public range land
       D. Increased vulnerability to forest fires due to under-
          use

23. Which of the following is a result of Turnell's decision   23.___
    to rotate his cattle?
       A. The production of cattle which tend to congregate
          less around water
       B. Increased bio-diversity which attracts and supports
          several animal species
       C. The production of beefier, more profitable cattle
       D. All of the above

24. Which of the following is an example of sustainable ranch-   24.___
    ing?
       A. The use of pesticides to control disease
       B. Non-use of, and non-reliance on, public grazing lands
       C. Rotation of cattle away from riparian areas
       D. Independent decision-making

25. Which of the following is an effect of the increased
    diversity of plant life on the grazing land that Turnell
    uses?
    A. Production of leaner cattle
    B. Production of larger, meatier cattle
    C. Production of more abundant but less nutritious
       grasses
    D. Less reliance on pesticides

25.___

KEY (CORRECT ANSWERS)

1. A		11. B	
2. D		12. C	
3. B		13. A	
4. C		14. A	
5. B		15. D	
6. B		16. B	
7. D		17. D	
8. A		18. A	
9. C		19. C	
10. B		20. B	

21. D
22. A
23. B
24. C
25. B

ARITHMETIC
EXAMINATION SECTION
TEST 1

DIRECTIONS: Each question or incomplete statement is followed by several suggested answers or completions. Select the one that *BEST* answers the question or completes the statement. *PRINT THE LETTER OF TEE CORRECT ANSWER IN THE SPACE AT THE RIGHT.*

1. Add $4.34, $34.50, $6.00, $101.76, $90.67. From the result, subtract $60.54 and $10,56.   1.____

    A. $76.17   B. $156.37   C. $166.17   D. $300.37

2. Add 2,200, 2,600, 252 and 47.96. From the result, subtract 202.70, 1,200, 2,150 and   2.____
434.43.

    A. 1,112.83   B. 1,213.46   C. 1,341.51   D. 1,348.91

3. Multiply 1850 by .05 and multiply 3300 by .08 and, then, add both results,   3.____

    A. 242.50   B. 264,00   C. 333.25   D. 356.50

4. Multiply 312.77 by .04. Round off the result to the nearest hundredth.   4.____

    A. 12.52   B. 12.511   C. 12.518   D. 12.51

5. Add 362.05, 91.13, 347.81 and 17.46 and then divide the result by 6. The answer,   5.____
rounded off to the nearest hundredth, is:

    A. 138.409   B. 137.409   C. 136.41   D. 136.40

6. Add 66.25 and 15.06 and,then,multiply the result by 2 1/6.   6.____
The answer is, most nearly,

    A. 176.18   B. 176.17   C. 162.66   D. 162.62

7. Each of the following items contains three decimals. In which case do *all* three decimals   7.____
have the *SAME* value?

    A. .3; .30; .03   B. .25; .250; .2500
    C. 1.9; 1.90;1.09   D. .35; .350; .035

8. Add 1/2 the sum of (539.84 and 479.26) to 1/3 the sum of (1461.93 and 927.27). Round   8.____
off the result to the nearest whole number.

    A. 3408   B. 2899   C. 1816   D. 1306

9. Multiply $5,906.09 by 15% and, then, divide the result by 3 and round off to the nearest   9.____
cent.

    A. $295.30   B. $885.91   C. $2,657.74   D. $29,530.45

10. Multiply 630 by 517.   10.____

    A. 325,710   B. 345,720   C. 362,425   D. 385,660

11. Multiply 35 by 846.   11.___

    A.   4050   B.   9450   C.   18740   D.   29610

12. Multiply 823 by 0.05.   12.___

    A.   0.4115   B.   4.115   C.   41.15   D.   411.50

13. Multiply 1690 by 0.10.   13.___

    A.   0.169   B.   .1.69   C.   16.90   D.   169.0

14. Divide 2765 by 35.   14.___

    A. 71   B. 79   C. 87   D. 93

15. From $18.55 subtract $6.80.   15.___

    A. $9.75   B. $10.95   C. $11.75   D. $25.35

16. The sum of 2.75 + 4.50 + 3.60 is: 16.___

    A. 9.75   B. 10.85   C. 11.15   D. 11.95

17. The sum of 9.63 + 11.21 + 17.25 is: 17.___

    A. 36.09   B. 38.09   C. 39.92   D. 41.22

18. The sum of 112.0 + 16.9 + 3.84 is: 18.___

    A. 129.3   B. 132.74   C. 136.48   D. 167.3

19. When 65 is added to the result of 14 multiplied by 13, the answer is: 19.___

    A. 92   B. 182   C. 247   D. 16055

20. From $391.55 subtract $273.45.   20.___

    A. $118.10   B. $128.20   C. $178.10   D. $218.20

KEY (CORRECT ANSWERS)

1.	C	11.	D
2.	A	12.	C
3.	D	13.	D
4.	D	14.	B
5.	C	15.	C
6.	B	16.	B
7.	B	17.	B
8.	D	18.	B
9.	C	19.	C
10.	A	20.	A

SOLUTIONS TO PROBLEMS

1. ($4.34 + $34.50 + $6.00 + $101.76 + $90.67) - ($60.54 + $10.56) = $237.27 - $71.10 = $166.17.

2. (2200 + 2600 + 252 + 47.96) - (202.70 + 1200 + 2150 + 434.43) = 5099.96 - 3987.13 = 1112.83

3. (1850)(.05) + (3300)(.08) = 92.5 + 264 = 356.50

4. (312.77)(.04) = 12.5108 = 12.51 to nearest hundredth

5. $(362.05 + 91.13 + 347.81 + 17.46) \div 6 = 136.408\overline{3} = 136.41$ to nearest hundredth

6. $(66.25 + 15.06)(2\frac{1}{6}) = 176.171\overline{6} \approx 176.17$

7. .25 = .250 = .2500

8. $(\frac{1}{2})(539.84 + 479.26) + \frac{1}{3}(1461.93 + 927.27) = 509.55 + 796.4 = 1305.95 = 1306$ nearest whole number

9. ($5906.09)(.15) ÷ 3 = ($885.9135)/3 = 295.3045 = $295.30 to nearest cent

10. (630)(517) = 325,710

11. (35)(846) = 29,610

12. (823)(.05) = 41.15

13. (1690)(10) = 169.0

14. 2765 ÷ 3.5 = 79

15. $18.55 - $6.80 = $11.75

16. 2.75 + 4.50 + 3.60 = 10.85

17. 9.63 + 11.21 + 17.25 = 38.09

18. 112.0 + 16.9 + 3.84 = 132.74

19. 65 + (14)(13) = 65 + 182 = 247

20. $391.55 - $273.45 = $118.10

TEST 2

DIRECTIONS   Each question or incomplete statement is followed by several suggested answers or completions. Select the one that *BEST* answers the question or completes the statement. *PRINT THE LETTER OF TEE CORRECT ANSWER IN THE SPACE AT THE RIGHT.*

1. The sum of $29.61 + $101.53 + $943.64 is: 1.___
    A. $983.88   B. $1074.78   C. $1174.98   D. $1341.42

2. The sum of $132.25 + $85.63 + $7056,44 is: 2.___
    A. $1694.19   B. $7274.32   C. $8464.57   D. $9346.22

3. The sum of 4010 + 1271 + 838 + 23 is: 3.___
    A. 6142   B. 6162   C. 6242   D. 6362

4. The sum of 53632 + 27403 + 98765 + 75424 is: 4.___
    A. 19214   B. 215214   C. 235224   D. 255224

5. The sum of 76342 + 49050 + 21206 + 59989 is: 5.___
    A. 196586   B. 206087   C. 206587   D. 234487

6. The sum of $452.13 + $963.45 + $621.25 is: 6.___
    A. $1936.83   B. $2036.83   C. $2095.73   D. $2135.73

7. The sum of 36392 + 42156 + 98765 is: 7.___
    A. 167214   B. 177203   C. 177313   D. 178213

8. The sum of 40125 + 87123 + 24689 is: 8.___
    A. 141827   B. 151827   C. 151937   D. 161947

9. The sum of 2379 + 4015 + 6521 + 9986 is: 9.___
    A. 22901   B. 22819   C. 21801   D. 21791

10. From 50962 subtract 36197.   10.___
    A. 14675   B. 14765   C. 14865   D. 24765

11. From 90000 subtract 31928.   11.___
    A. 58072   B. 59062   C. 68172   D. 69182

12. From 63764 subtract 21548.   12.___
    A. 42216   B. 43122   C. 45126   D. 85312

13. From $9605.13 subtract $2715.96.   13.___
    A. $12,321.09   B. $8,690.16   C. $6,990.07   D. $6,889.17

14. From 76421 subtract 73101.   14.____

    A.   3642   B.   3540   C.   3320   D.   3242

15. From $8.25 subtract $6.50.   15.____

    A. $1.25   B. $1.50   C. $1.75   D. $2.25

16. Multiply 583 by 0.50.   16.____

    A. $291.50   B. 28.15   C. 2.815   D. 0.2815

17. Multiply 0.35 by 1045.   17.____

    A. 0.36575   B. 3.6575   C. 36.575   D. 365.75

18. Multiply 25 by 2513.   18.____

    A. 62825   B. 62725   C. 60825   D. 52825

19. Multiply 423 by 0.01.   19.____

    A. 0.0423   B. 0.423   C. 4.23   D. 42.3

20. Multiply 6.70 by 3.2.   20.____

    A. 2.1440   B. 21.440   C. 214.40   D. 2144.0

KEY (CORRECT ANSWERS)

1.	B		11.	A
2.	B		12.	A
3.	A		13.	D
4.	D		14.	C
5.	C		15.	C
6.	B		16.	A
7.	C		17.	D
8.	C		18.	A
9.	A		19.	C
10.	B		20.	B

SOLUTIONS TO PROBLEMS

1. $29.61 + $101.53 + $943.64 = $1074.78

2. $132.25 + $85.63 + $7056.44 = $7274.32

3. 4010 + 1271 + 838 + 23 = 6142

4. 53,632 + 27,403 + 98,765 + 75,424 = 255,224

5. 76,342 + 49,050 + 21,206 + 59,989 = 206,587

6. $452.13 + $963.45 + $621.25 = $2036.83

7. 36,392 + 42,156 + 98,765 = 177,313

8. 40,125 + 87,123 + 24,689 = 151,937

9. 2379 + 4015 + 6521 + 9986 = 22,901

10. 50962 - 36197 = 14,765

11. 90,000 - 31,928 = 58,072

12. 63,764 - 21,548 = 42,216

13. $9605.13 - $2715.96 = $6889.17

14. 76,421 - 73,101 = 3320

15. $8.25 - $6.50 = $1.75

16. (583)(.50) = 291.50

17. (.35)(1045) = 365.75

18. (25)(2513) = 62,825

19. (423)(.01) = 4.23

20. (6.70)(3.2) = 21.44

TEST 3

DIRECTIONS : Each question or incomplete statement is followed by several suggested answers or completions. Select the one that *BEST* answers the question or completes the statement. *PRINT THE LETTER OF TEE CORRECT ANSWER IN THE SPACE AT THE RIGHT.*

Questions 1-4.

DIRECTIONS: For each of Questions 1-4, perform the indicated arithmetic and choose the correct answer from among the four choices given.

1. 12.485
    + 347

    A.   12,038   B.   12,128   C.   12,782   D.   12,832

2. 74,137
    + 711

    A.   74,326   B.   74,848   C.   78,028   D.   .D. 78,926

3. 3,749
    - 671

    A.   3,078   B.   3,168   C.   4,028   D.   4,420

4.   19,805
     -18904

    A.   109   B.   901   C.   1,109   D.   1,901

5. When 119 is subtracted from the sum of 2016 + 1634, the remainder is:

    A.   2460   B.   3531   C.   3650   D.   3769

6. Multiply 35 X 65 X 15.

    A.   2275   B.   24265   C.   31145   D.   34125

7. 90% expressed as a decimal is:

    A.   .009   B.   .09   C.   .9   D.   9.0

8. Seven-tenths of a foot expressed in inches is:

    A.   5.5   B.   6.5   C.   7   D.   8.4

9. If 95 men were divided into crews of five men each, the *number* of crews that will be formed is:

    A.   16   B.   17   C.   18   D.   19

1.____
2.____
3.____
4.____
5.____
6.____
7.____
8.____
9.____

10. If a man earns $19.50 an hour, the *number* of working hours it will take him to earn $4,875 is, most nearly,

   A. 225   B. 250   C. 275   D. 300

10.___

11. If 5 1/2 loads of gravel cost $55.00, then 6 1/2 loads will cost:

   A. $60.   B. $62.50   C. $65.   D. $66.00

11.___

12. At $2.50 a yard, 27 yards of concrete will cost:

   A. $36.   B. $41.80   C. $54.   D. $67.50

12.___

13. A distance is measured and found to be 52.23 feet. In feet and inches, this distance is, most nearly, 52 feet *and*

   A. 2 3/4"   B. 3 1/4"   C. 3 3/4"   D. 4 1/4"

13.___

14. If a maintainer gets $5.20 per hour and time and one-half for working over 40 hours, his *gross* salary for a week in which he worked 43 hours would be

   A. $208.00   B. $223.60   C. $231.40   D. $335.40

14.___

15. The circumference of a circle is given by the formula $C = \Pi D$, where C is the circumference, D is the diameter, and Π is about 3 1/7.
If a coil is 15 turns of steel cable has an average diameter of 20 inches, the *total* length of cable on the coil is *nearest to*

   A. 5 feet   B. 78 feet   C. 550 feet   D. 943 feet

15.___

16. The measurements of a poured concrete foundation show that 54 cubic feet of concrete have been placed.
If payment for this concrete is to be on the basis of cubic yards, the 54 cubic feet must be

   A. multiplied by 27   B. multiplied by 3
   C. divided by 27   D. divided by 3

16.___

17. If the cost of 4 1/2 tons of structural steel is $1,800, then the cost of 12 tons is, most nearly,

   A. $4,800   B. $5,400   C. $7,200   D. $216,000

17.___

18. An hourly-paid employee working 12:00 midnight to 8:00 a.m. is directed to report to the medical staff for a physical examination at 11:00 a.m. of the same day.
The pay allowed him for reporting will be an extra

   A. 1 hour   B. 2 hours   C. 3 hours   D. 4 hours

18.___

19. The *total* length of four pieces of 2" pipe, whose lengths are 7' 3 1/2", 4' 2 3/16", 5' 7 5/16", and 8' 5 7/8", respectively, is:

   A. 24' 6 3/4"   B. 24' 7 15/16"
   C. 25' 5 13/16"   D. 25' 6 7/8"

19.___

20. As a senior mortuary caretaker, you are preparing a monthly report, using the following   20._____
    figures:

    No. of bodies received   983
    No. of bodies claimed   720
    No. of bodies sent to city cemetery   14
    No. of bodies sent to medical schools   9

How many bodies remained at the end of the monthly reporting period?

  A.   230   B.   240   C.   250   D.   260

———

KEY (CORRECT ANSWERS)

1.	D	11.	C
2.	B	12.	D
3.	A	13.	A
4.	B	14.	C
5.	B	15.	B
6.	D	16.	C
7.	C	17.	A
8.	D	18.	C
9.	D	19.	D
10.	B	20.	B

———

SOLUTIONS TO PROBLEMS

1. $12,485 + 347 = 12,832$

2. $74,137 + 711 = 74,848$

3. $3749 - 671 = 3078$

4. $19,805 - 18,904 = 901$

5. $(2016 + 1634) - 119 = 3650 - 119 = 3531$

6. $(35)(65)(15) = 34,125$

7. $90\% = .90$ or $.9$

8. $(\frac{7}{10})(12) = 8.4$ inches

9. $95 \div 5 = 19$ crews

10. $\$4875 \div \$19.50 = 250$ days

11. Let x = cost. Then, $\dfrac{5\frac{1}{2}}{6\frac{1}{2}} = \dfrac{\$55.00}{x}$. $5\frac{1}{2} = 357.50$. Solving, $x = \$65$

12. $(\$2.50)(27) = \$67.50$

13. $.23$-ft.$=2.76$in., so 52.23ft ≈ 52 ft. $2\frac{3}{4}$in. $(.76 \approx \frac{3}{4})$

14. Salary $= (\$5.20)(40) + (\$7.80)(3) = \$231.40$

15. Length $\approx (15)(3\frac{1}{7})(20) \approx 943$ in. ≈ 78 ft.

16. There are 27 cu.ft. in 1 cu.yd. To change from 54 cu.ft. to cu.yds., divide by 27.

17. $\$1800 \div 4\frac{1}{2} = = \$400$ per ton. Then, 12 tons cost $(\$400)(12) = \$4800$

18. Instead of working 12 to 8, he will be staying until 11 AM, an extra 3 hours.

19. $7'3\frac{1}{2}" + 4'2\frac{3}{16}" + 5'7\frac{5}{16}" + 8'5\frac{7}{8}" = 24'17\frac{30}{16}" = 24'18\frac{7}{8}"$

20. $983 - 720 - 14 - 9 = 240$ bodies left.

———————

ARITHMETICAL REASONING
EXAMINATION SECTION
TEST 1

DIRECTIONS: Each question or incomplete statement is followed by several suggested answers or completions. Select the one that BEST answers the question or completes the statement. *PRINT THE LETTER OF THE CORRECT ANSWER IN THE SPACE AT THE RIGHT.*

1. A class decided to cultivate a garden. The principal gave them a piece of ground 40 feet   1.____
    long and 30 feet wide. There were 18 boys and 12 girls in the class. The class voted that
    each pupil should be allowed an equal amount of the space in the garden.
    The number of square feet which was set aside for the *exclusive* use of the boys was

    A. 30   B. 40   C. 480   D. 720

2. The chef allowed 20 minutes cooking time per pound for a roast weighing 6 lbs. 12 ozs. If   2.____
    the roast was placed in the oven at 4:20 P.M., it *should be done* by

    A. 6:00 P.M.   B. 6:32 P.M.   C. 6:35 P.M.   D. 7:12 P.M.

3. To check the correctness of the answer to a multiplication example, divide the   3.____

    A. product by the multiplier
    B. multiplier by the product
    C. multiplicand by the multiplier
    D. multiplier by the multiplicand

4. Of the following correct ways to solve .125 X .32, the MOST efficient is to   4.____

    A. write .125 under .32, multiply, point off 5 places
    B. write .32 under .125, multiply, point off 5 places
    C. multiply 125 by 32 and divide by 1000 X 100
    D. divide .32 by 8

5. If you were to eat each meal in a different restaurant in the city's eating places, assuming   5.____
    that you eat 3 meals a day, it would take you more than 19 years to cover all of the city's
    eating places.
    On the basis of this information, the BEST of the following choices is that the number
    of restaurants in the city

    A. exceeds 20,500   B. is closer to 21,000 than 22,000
    C. exceeds 21,000   D. does not exceed 21,500

6. The cost of electricity for operating an 875-watt toaster, an 1100-watt steam iron, and   6.____
    four 75-watt lamps, each for one hour, at 7.5 cents per kilowatt hour (1 kilowatt equals
    1000 watts) is

    A. 15 cents   B. 17 cents   C. $1.54   D. $1.71

7. Of the following, the pair that is NOT a set of equivalents is: 7.____

    A. .021%, .00021   B. 1/4%, .0025
    C. 1.5%, 3/200   D. 225%, .225

8. Assuming that the series will continue in the same pattern, the NEXT number in the series 3, 5, 11, 29.......is   8._____

   A. 41   B. 47   C. 65   D. 83

9. If the total area of a picture measuring 10 inches by 12 inches plus a matting of uniform width surrounding the picture is 224 square inches, the WIDTH of the matting is   9._____

   A. 2 inches   B. 2 4/11 inches   C. 3 inches   D. 4 inches

10. The *net price* of a $25 item after SUCCESSIVE discounts of 20% and 30% is   10._____

   A. $11   B. $12.50   C. $14   D. $19

KEY (CORRECT ANSWERS)

1. D	6. B
2. C	7. D
3. A	8. D
4. D	9. A
5. A	10. C

SOLUTIONS TO ARITHMETICAL REASONING

1. Answer: (D) 720

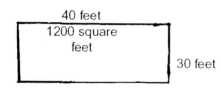

$\dfrac{40 \text{ sq.}}{30\sqrt{1200}}$ ft. per child

18 (boys) X 40 = 720 sq. ft.

2. Answer: (C) 6:35 P.M.

20 minutes for 1 lb.

$\begin{array}{r} 120 \\ + \ 15 \\ \hline 135 \text{ minutes} \\ -120 \text{ minutes (2 hours)} \\ \hline 15 \text{ minutes} \end{array}$

$\therefore \dfrac{12 \text{ oz.}}{16 \text{ oz.}} = \dfrac{3}{4} \text{ lb.}$

3/4 X 20 = 15 minutes
20 X 6   = 120 minutes

$\begin{array}{r} 4:20 \text{ P.M.} \\ + \ 2:15 \text{ (2 hours, 15 minutes)} \\ \hline 6:35 \text{ P.M.} \end{array}$

3. Answer: (A) product by the multiplier

$\begin{array}{r} 12 \text{ (multiplicand)} \\ \times \ 2 \text{ (multiplier)} \\ \hline 24 \text{ (product)} \end{array}$

4. Answer: (D) divide .32 by 8
   The most efficient way is to divide .32 by 8.
   .125= .12 1/2 = 12 1/2% = 1/8

   $1/8 \times .32 = \dfrac{.32}{8}$

   $\begin{array}{r} .04 \\ 8\overline{).32} \\ \underline{.32} \end{array}$

5. Answer: (A) exceeds 20,500

        365 (days in 1 year)
     ×   3 (meals)
     ‾‾‾‾‾‾‾‾
       1095 (meals in 1 year)
     ×   19 (number of years)
     ‾‾‾‾‾‾‾‾
       20,805 (number of meals eaten in 19 years)
     +   12 (number of meals eaten in leap years)
     ‾‾‾‾‾‾‾‾
       20,817 (total)

            4 (leap-year days)
        ×   3 (meals)
        ‾‾‾‾‾‾‾
           12 (leap-year meals)

6. Answer: (B) 17 cents
    875 + 1100 + 300 = 2275 watts
    2275 / 1000 = 2 11/40 kilowatt hours
    2 11/40 x 7.5 cents = $.17 approximately

7. Answer: (D) 225%, .225
    Taking each alternative in turn:

    A. .021% = .00021

    B. $1/4\% = \dfrac{1}{400} = .0025$

    C. $1.5\% = .015 + \dfrac{15}{1000} = \dfrac{3}{200}$

    D. 225% = 2.25 (not .225)

8. Answer: (D) 83
    ### SUGGESTIONS FOR SERIES PROBLEMS
    1. Find the differences between the numbers (or squares of differences).
    2. In this series, each difference is multiplied by 3 and added to the succeeding number.
        3,5:   the difference is 2; this difference was multiplied by 3, giving 6, which was then added to 5, to make the next number in the series 11.
        5,11:   the difference is 6; this difference was multiplied by 3, giving 18, which was then added to 11, to make the next number in the series 29.
        11,29: the difference is 18; this difference should be multiplied by 3, giving 54, which, when added to 29, will give the next number in the series, 83.

9. Answer: (A) 2 inches

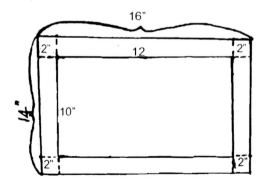

The total area = 224 square inches (16 x 14).
If 2 inches are added to either side of the picture's width and to either side of the picture's length, we get a new width of 14 inches (10+4) and a new length of 16 inches (12+4). Therefore, 14 x 16 = 224 square inches.
Or, a uniform matting width of 2 inches.

10. Answer: (C) $14
    SOLUTION

ALTERNATE SOLUTION

Successful discounts
    20%, 30%

1. Convert to decimals .2, .3
2. Subtract from 1.0 .8, .7
3. Multiply .8 X .7 = .56
4. 1.00 - .56 = .44

$$
\begin{array}{r}
25.00 \\
\times \quad .44 \\
\hline
100 \\
100 \\
\hline
\$11.00
\end{array}
$$

5. $25.00 - $11.00 = $14.00

$$
\begin{array}{r}
\$ 25 \\
\times \quad .20 \\
\hline
\$ 5
\end{array}
$$

$25 - $5 = $20

$$
\begin{array}{r}
\$20 \\
\times \quad .30 \\
\hline
\$ 6
\end{array}
$$

$20 - $6 = $14

TEST 2

DIRECTIONS: Each question or incomplete statement is followed by several suggested answers or completions. Select the one that BEST answers the question or completes the statement. *PRINT THE LETTER OF THE CORRECT ANSWER IN THE SPACE AT THE RIGHT.*

1. The cost of 63 inches of ribbon at 12 cents per yard is   1.___

    A. $.20   B. $.21   C. $.22   D. $.23

2. If 1 1/2 cups of cereal are used with 4 1/2 cups of water, the amount of water needed with   2.___
3/4 of a cup of cereal is

    A. 2 cups   B. 2 1/8 cups   C. 2 1/4 cups   D. 2 1/2 cups

3. Under certain conditions, sound travels at about 1100 ft. per second. If 88 ft. per second   3.___
is approximately equivalent to 60 miles per hour, the speed of sound, under the above
conditions, is, of the following, *closest to*

    A. 730 miles per hour   B. 740 miles per hour
    C. 750 miles per hour   D. 760 miles per hour

4. Of the following, the *most nearly* accurate set of equivalents is: 4.___

    A. 1 ft. equals 30.48 centimeters
    B. 1 centimeter equals 2.54 inches
    C. 1 rod equals 3.28 meters
    D. 1 meter equals 1.09 feet

5. If one angle of a triangle is three times a second angle and the third angle is 20 degrees   5.___
more than the second angle, the SECOND ANGLE is

    A. 32°   B. 34°   C. 40°   D. 50°

6. Assuming that on a blueprint 1/4 inch equals 12 inches, the *actual* length in feet of a steel   6.___
bar represented on the blueprint by a line 3 3/8 inches long is

    A. 3 3/8   B. 6 3/4   C. 12 1/2   D. 13 1/2

7. A plane leaves Denver, Colorado, on June 1st at 1 P.M. Mountain Standard Time and   7.___
arrives at New York City on June 2nd at 2 A.M. Eastern Daylight Saving Time. The *actual*
time of flight was

    A. 10 hours   B. 11 hours   C. 12 hours   D. 13 hours.

8. Of the following, the value *closest to* that of $\dfrac{42.10 \times .0003}{.002}$ is: 8.___

    A. .063   B. .63   C. 6.3   D. 63

9. If Mrs. Jones bought 3 3/4 yards of dacron at $1.16 per yard and 4 2/3 yards of velvet at   9.___
$3.87 per yard, the amount of change she receives from $25 is

    A. $2.12   B. $2.28   C. $2.59   D. $2.63

10. The water level of a swimming pool, 75 feet by 42 feet, is to be raised 4 inches. The num- 10.____
ber of gallons of water needed for this purpose is (1 cubic foot equals 7 1/2 gallons)

   A. 140   B. 7,875   C. 31,500   D. 94,500

KEY (CORRECT ANSWERS)

1. B	6. D
2. C	7. A
3. C	8. C
4. A	9. C
5. A	10. B

SOLUTIONS TO ARITHMETICAL REASONING

1. Answer: (B) $.21
   SOLUTION

   $$63'' = \frac{63}{36} \text{ yds}; \quad \frac{\overset{21}{\cancel{63}}}{\cancel{36}} \times \frac{.01}{\cancel{.12}} = 21¢$$

   ALTERNATE SOLUTION

   12¢ per yard

   $$\frac{12}{36} = \frac{1}{3} ¢ \text{ per inch}; \quad \frac{63''}{1} \times \frac{1}{3} ¢ = \frac{63}{3} = 21¢$$

2. Answer: (C) 2 1/4 cups SOLUTION

Proportion	Cereal	Water
1st mixture	1 1/2 cups	4 1/2 cups
2nd mixture	3/4 cups	x cups

   3/4 is half of 1 1/2; therefore, half of 4 1/2 is 1/4

   ALTERNATE SOLUTION

   From the data given, we form the proportion,
   1 1/2(cups of cereal): 4 1/2 (cups of water)=3/4 (cup of cereal):x

   ∴ 3/2 : 9/2 = 3/4 : x
   3/2x = 27/4
     x = 9/4 - 2 1/4 (cups of water)

3. Answer: (C) 750 miles per hour
   Speed of sound = 1100 ft. per second
   88 ft. per second = 60 miles an hour

   $$\frac{1100}{88} = 12\ 1/2 \text{ (the number of times the speed of sound is greater than 60 miles an hour)}$$

   ∴ 60 x 12 1/2 = 750 miles per hour (the speed of sound)

4. Answer: (A) 1 ft. equals 30.48 centimeters
   Taking each alternative in turn:
   1. A meter = 100 centimeters
      A meter = 39 in. (approx.) = 3 1/4 ft. (39/12 = 3 1/4)

      3 1/4 ft. =1 meter = 100 centimeters

      $$∴ 1 \text{ ft.} = \frac{100}{3\ 1/4} = 30.48 \text{ centimeters (approx.)}$$
   2. 1 meter = 39 in. = 3 1/4 ft. (approx.)
   3. 1 centimeter = .39 in.
   4. 1 rod = 5.1/2 yds. = 16 1/2 ft.

      ∴ 1 rod = 5 meters (approx.) (see Item 2 above)

5. Answer: (A) 32°
Let x = second angle
Let 3x = first angle
Let x + 20° = third angle
∴ 5x + 20 = 180°
   x = 32°

6. Answer: (D) 13 1/2

$$\frac{1/4''}{12} = \frac{3\ 3/8''}{x}$$

1/4 ÷ 12/1 = 27/8 ÷ x /1

1/4 X 1/12 = 27/8 X 1/x

$$\frac{1}{4} = \frac{27}{8x}$$
8x = 48 x 27 = 1296
   x = 162 inches
   = 13 1/2 ft.

7. Answer: (A) 10 hours
TIME BELTS

4 A. M. 5 A. M. 6 A. M. 7 A. M. E. S. T.
8 A.M. D.S.T.

In traveling eastward we set our clocks forward for each time zone.

Plane left at 1 P.M.
Traveled around clock 12 hours or 13 hours at 2 A.M.

Subtract 2 hours' difference between Mountain Time and Eastern Standard Time. Subtract another hour for Daylight Saving Time. That is, 13 - 3 = 10 hours

8. Answer: (C) 6.3
In 42.10, discard for practical purposes the .10 and perform as

follows: $\frac{42 \times .0003}{.002} = \frac{.0126}{.002} = \frac{12.6}{2} = 6.3$

9. Answer: (C) $2.59

$1.16		$3.87		$18.06		$25.00
× 3 3/4		× 4 2/3		+ 4.35		- 22.41
$4.35		$18.06		$22.41		$ 2.59

10. Answer: (B) 7,875
42 X 75 X 1/3 ft. (4") = 1050 cu. ft.

× 7 1/2
7,875 gallons

TEST 3

DIRECTIONS: Each question or incomplete statement is followed by several suggested answers or completions. Select the one that BEST answers the question or completes the statement. *PRINT THE LETTER OF THE CORRECT ANSWER IN THE SPACE AT THE RIGHT.*

1. The part of the total quantity represented by a 24-degree sector of a circle graph is   1.____

   A. 6 2/3%   B. 12%   C. 13 1/3%   D. 24%

2. If the shipping charges to a certain point are 62 cents for the first 5 oz. and 8 cents for   2.____
   each additional ounce, the weight of a package for which the charges are $1.66 is

   A. 13 ounces   B. 1 1/8 lbs.   C. 1 1/4 lbs.   D. 1 1/2 lbs.

3. If 15 cans of food are needed for 7 men for 2 days, the number of cans needed for 4 men   3.____
   for 7 days is

   A. 15   B. 20   C. 25   D. 30

4. The total saving in purchasing thirty 13-cent ice cream pops for a class party at a   4.____
   reduced rate of $1.38 per dozen is

   A. 35¢   B. 40¢   C. 45¢   D. 50¢

5. The quotient for the division of 36 apples among 4 children may be correctly found by   5.____
   thinking

   A. 36 ÷ 1/4   B. $36\overline{)4.0}$ C. 1/4 of 36   D. 4/36

6. The *missing term* in the equation: 1/3 of ? = 1/2 of 90 is   6.____

   A. 45   B. 30   C. 15   D. 135

7. The fraction *closest to* 4/5 is   7.____

   A. 2/3   B. 7/9   C. 8/11   D. 5/8

8. Of the following, the one which may be used CORRECTLY to compute the value of 4 X   8.____
   22 1/2 is:

   A. (4X45) + (4X1/2)   B. (4X1/2) + (4X2) + (4X2)
   C. (1/2 of 4) + (2X4) + (2X4)   D. (4X20) + (4X2) + (4X1/2)

9. 16 1/2 ÷ 1/4 may CORRECTLY be expressed as   9.____

   A. (1/4X16) + (1/4X1/2)   B. (4X16) + (4X1/2)
   C. $4\overline{)16.5}$ D. 1/4 times 33/2

10. In computation, 3/4 may be CORRECTLY transformed into 6/8 for the *same* reason that   10.____

    A. 7 (3 + 4) = 21 + 28   B. 3 apples + 5 apples = 8
    C. $.2\overline{)3.4}\ =\ 2\overline{)34}$ D. 3 + 4 = 4 + 3

KEY (CORRECT ANSWERS)

1. A	6. D
2. B	7. B
3. D	8. D
4. C	9. B
5. C	10. C

SOLUTIONS TO ARITHMETICAL REASONING

1. Answer: (A) 6 2/3%

$$\frac{24}{360} = \frac{2}{30} = \frac{1}{15} = .06 \ 2/3 = 6 \ 2/3\%$$

2. Answer: (B) 1 1/8 lbs.
    Total charges   = $1.66

    Charge for 1st 5 oz. = $\frac{.62}{\$1.04}$ (remaining charges at rate of .08/oz.)

    5 oz. + 13 oz. = 18 oz. (Total no. of oz. in weight of pkge.)

    OR $\frac{18}{16}$ = 1 1/8 lb.

3. Answer: (D) 30
    If 15 cans of food are needed for 7 men for 2 days, therefore,
    7 1/2 cans are needed for these same 7 men for 1 day.
    7 1/2 ÷ 7 = 15/ 14 the no. of cans needed by 1 man for 1 day.
    4 x 7 x 15/ 14 = 30, the number of cans needed by 4 men for 7 days.

4. Answer: (C) 45¢
    $.13 x 30 = $3.90 (regular rate)
    30 = 2 1/2 doz.; $1.38 x 2 1/2 = $3.45 (reduced rate)
    Total saving = $.45 ($3.90 - $3.45)

5. Answer: (C) 1/4 of 36   36/ 4 = 9

6. Answer: (D) 135   1/3 of ? = 1/2 of 90
$$1/3 \, x = 45$$
$$x = 3 \times 45$$
$$= 135$$

7. Answer: (B) 7/9   4/5 = .80   8/11 = .73
                      2/3 = .66   5/8 = .63
                      7/9 = .78

8. Answer: (D) (4 X 20) + (4 X 2) + (4 X 1/2)

   22 1/2
   × 4
   ───
   80   Choice (D) $(4 \times 20)+(4 \times 2)+(4 \times 1/2) = 80+8+2 = 90$
    8   (This is an example of the Distributive Law,
    2   which links the operations of addition and
   ───
   90   multiplication.)

9. Answer: (B) (4 X 16) + (4 X 1/2)

   $$16 \; 1/2 \div 4 = \frac{16 \; 1/2}{4} = 16 \; 1/2 \times 4/1 = (4 \times 16) + (4 \times 1/2)$$

10. Answer: (C) $2\overline{)3.4} = 2\overline{)\,34}$

   $$\frac{3}{4} = \frac{6}{8} \; ; \; \frac{3.4}{.2} = \frac{34}{2} = 17$$

TEST 4

DIRECTIONS: Each question or incomplete statement is followed by several suggested answers or completions. Select the one that BEST answers the question or completes the statement. *PRINT THE LETTER OF THE CORRECT ANSWER IN THE SPACE AT THE RIGHT.*

1. The mathematical law of distribution is illustrated by all of the following EXCEPT: 1.____

A.
```
   15
  X12
  150
   30
  180
```
B.
```
   15
  X12
   30
  150
  180
```
C.
```
   15
  X12
  180
```
D.
```
   15
  X12
   30
   15
  180
```

2. Of the following series of partial sums which might arise in the addition of 36 and 25, the   2.____
    one that is INCORRECT is:

A. 11, 31, 61   B. 11, 4, 6, 61   C. 11, 41, 61   D. 36, 56, 61

3. Of the following, the one which equals one million is: 3.____

A. ten hundred thousand
C. 10X10X10X10X10X10X10
B. 10^7
D. 1 plus 6 zeros

4. Of the following groups, the one containing four terms all associated with one algorismic   4.____
    process is:

A. Addend, quotient, dividend, divisor
B. Dividend, quotient, divisor, minuend
C. Dividend, quotient, addend, minuend
D. Multiplicand, product, minuend, addend

5. Depreciation of a certain machine is estimated, for any year, at 20% of its value at the   5.____
    beginning of the year. If the machine is purchased for $600, its estimated net value at the
    end of two years is *closest to*

A. $325   B. $350   C. $375   D. $400

6. Hats are purchased at the rate of $33 per dozen. If they are sold at a close-out sale for   6.____
    $2.50 each, the *percent loss* on the cost price is

A. 3   B. 3 1/3   C. 9 1/11   D. 10

7. The time, 3 hours, 58 minutes after 10:56 A.M., is   7.____

A. 4:54 P.M.   B. 2:54 P.M.   C. 4:15 P.M.   D. 2:15 P.M.

8. Mr. Brown had $20.00 when he took his three children on a bus trip. He spent $7.33 for   8.____
    the four tickets and bought each of the children a magazine costing 15¢, a candy bar
    costing 11¢, and a 5¢ package of chewing gum.
    His CHANGE from the $20.00 was

A. $12.74   B. $11.43   C. $11.74   D. $12.84

9. The loan value on a life insurance policy at the end of 5 years is $30.19 per $1000 of insurance. The LARGEST amount to the *nearest* dollar that can be borrowed on a $5500 policy at the end of five years is

    A. $17   B. $151   C. $166   D. $1660

9._____

10. Using cups that hold six ounces of milk, the number of cupfuls a person can obtain from 1 1/2 gallons of milk is

    A. 16   B. 24   C. 32   D. 64

10._____

KEY (CORRECT ANSWERS)

1. C	6. C
2. B	7. B
3. A	8. C
4. B	9. C
5. C	10. C

SOLUTIONS TO ARITHMETICAL REASONING

1. Answer: (C)

    $$\begin{array}{r} 15 \\ \times 12 \\ \hline 180 \end{array}$$

    (A) $\begin{array}{r} 10 \times 15 = 150 \\ 2 \times 15 = \ \ 30 \\ \hline 180 \end{array}$ (B) $\begin{array}{r} 2 \times 15 = \ \ 30 \\ 10 \times 15 = 150 \\ \hline 180 \end{array}$ (D) $\begin{array}{r} 2 \times 15 = \ \ 30 \\ 10 \times 15 = 15(0) \\ \hline 180 \end{array}$

    The Distributive Law links the operations of addition and arithmetic.

2. Answer: (B) 11, 4, 6, 61
    Partial Sums

    $\begin{array}{r} 36 \\ +25 \\ \hline 61 \end{array}$ (A) $\begin{array}{r} 11 \\ +20 \\ \hline 31 \\ +30 \\ \hline 61 \end{array}$ (C) $\begin{array}{r} 11 \\ +30 \\ \hline 41 \\ +20 \\ \hline 61 \end{array}$ (D) $\begin{array}{r} 36 \\ + 20 \\ \hline 56 \\ + \ 5 \\ \hline 61 \end{array}$

3. Answer: (A) ten hundred thousand 100,000 X 10 = 1,000,000

4. Answer: (B) dividend, quotient, divisor, minuend
    Division is repeated subtraction

    divisor $\begin{array}{r} 21 \\ 12\overline{)256} \\ 24 \\ \hline 16 \\ 12 \\ \hline 4 \end{array}$ quotient
    dividend

    16   minuend - partial dividend

    4   partial dividend

    $\begin{array}{r} 36 \\ \times 45 \\ \hline 180 \\ 144 \\ \hline 1620 \end{array}$ multiplicand
    multiplier
    partial product
    partial product
    product

    $\begin{array}{r} 5 \\ +6 \\ \hline 11 \end{array}$ addend
    addend
    sum

    $\begin{array}{r} 7,485 \\ 2,648 \\ \hline 4,837 \end{array}$ minuend
    subtrahend
    remainder (difference)

5. Answer: (C) $375

    $\begin{array}{r} \$600 \\ \times \ \ .20 \\ \hline 120.00 \end{array}$ $\begin{array}{r} \$480 \\ \times \ \ .20 \\ \hline 96.00 \end{array}$ $\begin{array}{r} \$600 \\ -120 \\ \hline \$480 \end{array}$ $\begin{array}{r} \$480 \\ - \ \ 96 \\ \hline \$384 \end{array}$ (approximately)

6. Answer: (C) 9 1/11
   Cost of one dozen

   Selling price of one dozen $33.00 $2.50
                                  30.00   × 12
                                $ 3.00 $30.00 sold at close-out sale

   $$\frac{L}{C} = \frac{\$\,3}{\$\,33} = \frac{1}{11} = 9\ 1/11\%$$

7. Answer: (B) 2:54 p.m.
   A simple way to do this is to add 4 minutes to 10:56 a.m., making 11:00 a.m. Adding 3 hours = 2:00 p.m.
   Adding 54 minutes (instead of 58 minutes, to compensate for the 4 minutes added to 10:56 a.m.) =2:54 p.m.

8. Answer: (C) $11.74

15¢	31¢	$7.33	$20.00
11¢	× 3	+ .93	- 8.26
5¢	93¢	$8 .26	$11.74
31¢			

   $8.26

9. Answer: (C) $166
   $30.19 x 5 = $150.95 (loan value on $5,00 policy at end of 5 yrs.)
   $150.95 ÷ 10 = $15.10 (approx.) (loan value on additional $500 at end of 5 years)
   ∴ $150.95 + $15.10 = $166 (approx.)

10. Answer: (C) 32
    We must know that 1 cup = 8 oz. and that 1 qt. = 4 cups or 32 oz.
    Since 1 gal. = 4 qts., 1 gal. = 128 oz. (4 x 32 oz.)
    ∴ 1/2 gal. = 64 oz. and 1 1/2 gal. = 192 oz. (128 + 64)

    Finally, 192 ÷ 6 = 32 (cups)

TEST 5

DIRECTIONS: Each question or incomplete statement is followed by several suggested answers or completions. Select the one that BEST answers the question or completes the statement. *PRINT THE LETTER OF THE CORRECT ANSWER IN THE SPACE AT THE RIGHT.*

1. A storekeeper purchased an article for $36. In order to include 10% of cost for overhead and to provide $9 of net profit, the MARKUP *should be*

    A. 25%   B. 35%   C. 37 1/2%   D. 40%

1.____

2. A rectangular carton has twice the height, one-third the length, and four times the width of a second carton. The *ratio* of the volume of the first carton to that of the second is

    A. 16:3   B. 3:1   C. 8:3   D. 3:8

2.____

3. If a boy has a number of dimes and quarters in his pocket adding up to $3.10, the LARGEST possible number of dimes he can have is

    A. 16   B. 28   C. 26   D. 21

3.____

4. In a number system using the base 10, the value represented by the first digit 3 reading from the left, in the number 82,364,371, is

    A. 30 times the value represented by the second digit 3
    B. 100 times the value represented by the second digit 3
    C. 1,000 times the value represented by the second digit 3
    D. 10,000 times the value represented by the second digit 3

4.____

5. The number of revolutions made by a bicycle wheel of 28-inch diameter in traveling 1/2 mile is *closest to*

    A. 720   B. 180   C. 360   D. 120

5.____

6. Of the following, the property which is *true* of ALL parallelograms is that the

    A. diagonals are equal
    B. diagonals meet at right angles
    C. sum of the interior angles is 180°
    D. diagonals bisect each other

6.____

7.
```
      218
  32)6985
      64
      58
      32
     265
     256
       9
```

Of the following explanations about steps in the above computation, the one which is LEAST meaningful or accurate is that the

7.____

A. 64 represents 200 X 32
B. 265 is the result of subtracting 320 from 585
C. 9 is part of the quotient
D. 256 symbolizes the subtraction of 32 eight times

8. Assuming that a system of meridians and parallels of latitude like that used on maps of the earth's surface, were designed for the moon's surface, the distance covered by a man traveling 1° on the moon, as compared to that covered in traveling 1° on the earth, would be

    8.____

A. equal
B. less
C. greater
D. sometimes greater and sometimes less

9. 1958 may MOST correctly be expressed in Roman numerals as

    9.____

  A. MDCDLVIII   B. CMMLVIII   C. MCMLVIII   D. MCMLIIX

10. If the *same* positive quantity is added to both the numerator and the denominator of a proper fraction, the VALUE of the new fraction as compared to that of the original fraction will be

    10.____

A. greater
C. equal
B. less
D. either greater or less

KEY (CORRECT ANSWERS)

1. B   6. D
2. C   7. C
3. C   8. B
4. C   9. C
5. C   10. A

SOLUTIONS TO ARITHMETICAL REASONING

1. Answer: (B) 35%
   Cost = $36
   Overhead = 10% of Cost, OR $3.60
   Profit = $9.00 (Given)
   Selling Price = $48.60 (36 + 3.60 + 9)
   Markup = $12.60 (48.60 (S.P.) - 36 (Cost))

   Finally $\dfrac{12.60 (\text{markup})}{36.00 (\text{cost})}$ = 35%

2. Answer: (C) 8:3

   1st carton
   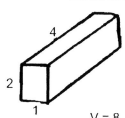
   V = 8

   2nd carton
   V = 3

   $\dfrac{V1}{V2} = \dfrac{8}{3}$

3. Answer: (C) 26   26 X 10 = $2.60 + .50 = $3.10

4. Answer: (C) 1,000 times the value represented by the second digit 3 (approximately) 300 x 1,000 = 300,000

5. Answer: (C) 360   C = π D
                            C = 22/ 7 X 28 = 88"

   1 revolution of wheel covers 88"
   1/2 X 5280 X 12/1 = traveling distance in inches

   6 X 5280 - 31680 inches

   ```
            360 revolutions
   88) 31680
       264
       528
       528
   ```

6. Answer: (D) diagonals bisect each other

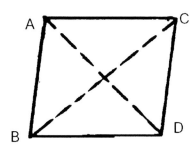

triangle = 180 °

parallelogram = 360°

7. Answer: (C) 9 is part of the quotient
    Division is repeated subtraction.
    Below is a division "pyramid," which shows what actually happens
    when we divide.

```
        8
       10
      200
  32)6985  dividend        32×100=3200
     6400                  32×200=6400
      585  partial dividend 32× 10=  320
      320
      265  partial dividend
      256
        9  partial dividend
```

8. Answer: (B) less
    Diameter of moon = 2000 miles ; Diameter of earth = 8000 miles

Moon

Earth

The larger the circle, the
larger the arc.

1° of arc = 1/360 of circle

Circumference of earth = 25,000 miles
Circumference of moon = 6,200 miles (1/4 of earth)

```
        69+
  360)25,000
      21 6              1° =69+miles on the equator (Earth)
      3 40             1° =17+miles (Moon)
      3 24
        16
```

9. Answer: (C) MCMLVIII

$$\begin{aligned} M &= 1000 \\ CM &= 900 \\ L &= 50 \\ VIII &= 8 \\ \hline &1958 \end{aligned}$$

10. Answer: (A) greater

$$\frac{2+2}{3+2} = \frac{4}{5} = \frac{12}{15}$$

$$\frac{2}{3} = \frac{10}{15}$$

INTERPRETING STATISTICAL DATA
GRAPHS, CHARTS AND TABLES

DIRECTIONS FOR THIS SECTION: Study the following graphs, charts, and/or tables. Base your answers to the questions that follow SOLELY on the information contained therein. *PRINT THE LETTER OF THE CORRECT ANSWER IN THE SPACE AT THE RIGHT.*

TEST 1

Questions 1-5.

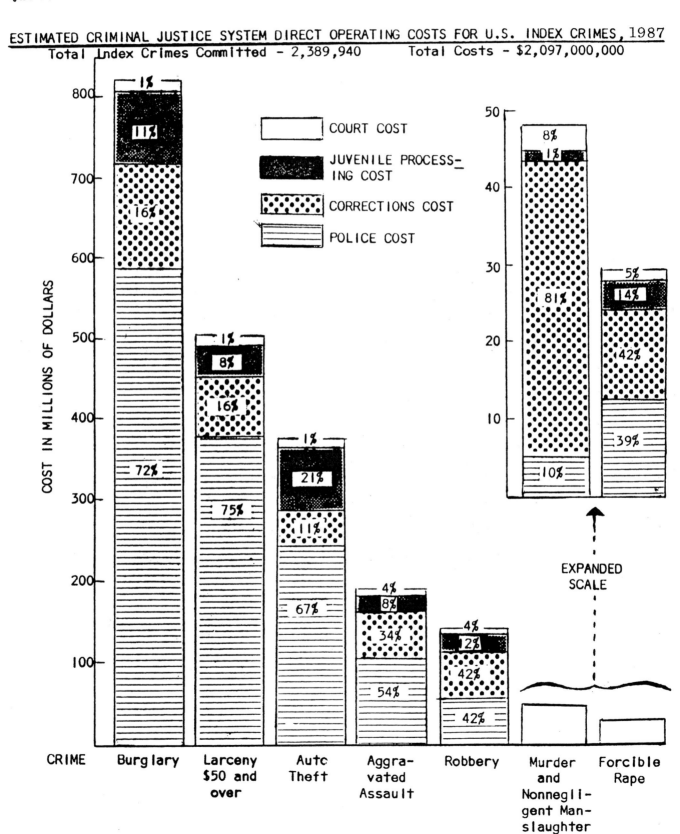

ESTIMATED CRIMINAL JUSTICE SYSTEM DIRECT OPERATING COSTS FOR U.S. INDEX CRIMES, 1987

Total Index Crimes Committed - 2,389,940   Total Costs - $2,097,000,000

NUMBER	1,000,000	625,000	407,000	206,000	118,000	9,850	22,470
PERCENT	42%	26%	17%	8½%	5%	½%	1%
DOLLARS (millions)	$820	$500	$370	$190	$140	$48	$29

1. According to the graph, which one of the following is *most nearly* the TOTAL AMOUNT of court costs for *all* U.S. index crimes in 1987?   1. ...
   A. $20,970,000   B. $35,390,000   C. $71,906,000
   D. $353,000,000
   E. the total cannot be determined from the information given

2. According to the graph, for which one of the following index crimes was the GREATEST amount of money spent on correction costs?   2. ...
   A. Larceny   B. Burglary   C. Auto theft
   D. Aggravated assault D. Murder and nonnegligent manslaughter

3. A certain administrator desires to determine for the crime of murder and nonnegligent manslaughter how much money was spent as juvenile processing costs per 1,000 crimes committed. Which *one* of the following formulas is MOST appropriate for determining that cost, according to the graph?   3. ...
   A. $\dfrac{.01 \times \$48,000,000}{9,850} \times 1,000$ B. $\dfrac{.01 \times \$48,000}{1,000} \times 9,850$
   C. $\dfrac{.01 \times \$48,000,000}{9,850} \div 1,000$ D. $\dfrac{.01 \times 9,850}{1,000} \times \$48,000,000$
   E. $\dfrac{.01 \times 1,000}{9,850} \div \$48,000,000$

4. According to the graph, which *one* of the following choices *most nearly* states the PROPORTIONATE RELATIONSHIP between the police cost per crime committed for burglary, per crime committed for larceny, and per crime committed for auto theft?   4. ...
   The proportionate relationship
   A. is approximately .97 to .985 to 1.0
   B. is approximately 1.0 to 1.04 to .93
   C. is approximately 6.00 to 3.75 to 2.50
   D. is approximately 1.00 to .97 to 1.10
   E. cannot be determined from the data in the graph

5. According to the graph, which *one* of the following kinds of crime has the GREATEST cost per crime?   5. ...
   A. Forcible rape   B. Robbery   C. Burglary
   D. Aggravated assault   E. Murder and nonnegligent manslaughter

TEST 2

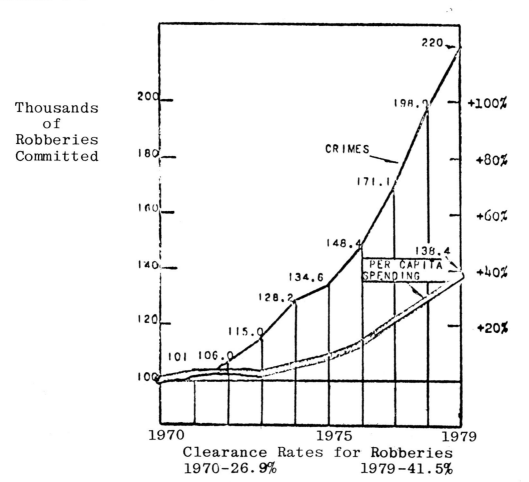

1. Which *one* of the following is MOST NEARLY the increase in   1. ...
   robberies from 1970 to 1979
      A. 12.0   B. 21.1   C. 120.0   D. 211.0   E. 120,000.0

2. Which *one* of the following choices MOST ACCURATELY compares 2. ...
   the percentage change between 1970 and 1979 in the number of
   robberies cleared, the number of robberies committed, and the
   per capital spending? *The percentage increase in the number of*
   robberies cleared is
      A. GREATER THAN *both* the percentage increase in robberies
         committed and the percentage increase in per capita
         spending
      B. LESS THAN *both* the percentage increase in robberies com-
         mitted and the percentage increase in per capita spending
      C. GREATER THAN the percentage increase in per capita spend-
         ing and LESS THAN the percentage increase in robberies
         committed
      D. GREATER THAN the percentage increase in robberies commit-
         ted and LESS THAN the percentage increase in per capita
         spending
      E. ABOUT THE SAME AS the percentage increase in per capita
         spending and LESS THAN the percentage incease in robberies
         committed

3

3. In which one of the following years did the GREATEST in- 3. ...
   increase occur in thousands of robberies committed? In
   A. 1974, in comparison with 1973
   B. 1976, in comparison with 1975
   C. 1977, in comparison with 1976
   D. 1978, in comparison with 1977
   E. 1979, in comparison with 1978

TEST 3

Questions 1-3.

MONTHS IN 1975 COMPARED WITH THE SAME MONTHS IN 1974

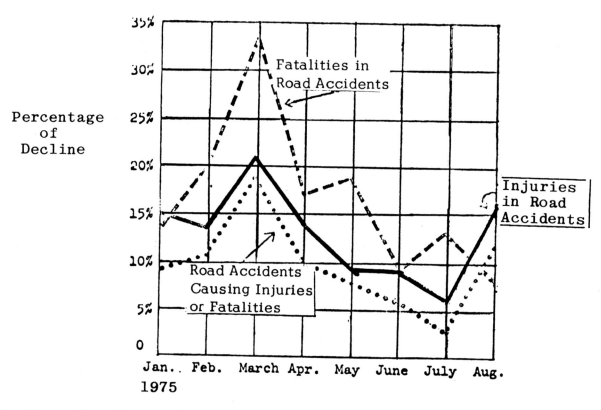

1. From the chart, it is possible to compare the number of 1. ...
   fatalities in any month of 1974 with the same month in 1975.
   Which *one* of the following statements is the MOST ACCURATE
   comparison? The number of fatalities in
   A. each month in 1975 was *less than* the same month in 1974
   B. each month in 1975 was *more than* the same month in 1974
   C. 1975 was *less than* the same month in 1974 only in the
      months of March, May, and July
   D. 1975 was *more than* the same month in 1974 only in the
      months of March, May, and July
   E. 1975 was *less than* the same month in 1974 only in the
      months of January, April, June, and August
2. If the ratio of fatalities to road accidents causing injuries 2. ...
   or fatalities in July,1974,was one fatality to 10 such road ac-
   cidents,which *one* of the following,if any,can be determined to
   be the RATIO of fatalities to road accidents in July,1975?
   A. One fatality to about 15 road accidents
   B. One fatality to about 11 road accidents

C. One fatality to about 9 road accidents
D. 12 fatalities to about 3 road accidents
E. The 1975 ratio cannot be determined from the facts given
3. Based on the graph, in which one of the following months of   3. ...
1975 did the GREATEST percentage improvement occur in the number of road fatalities, in comparison with the same month of
the previous year?
   A. May   B. June   C. July   D. April   E. August

TEST 4

Questions 1-8.
DIRECTIONS: The following graph shows expenses in five selected categories for a one-year period, expressed as percentages of these same
expenses during the previous year. The graph compares two different
offices. In Office T (represented by ▨▨▨▨▨▨▨) a cost reduction
program has been tested for the past year. The other office, Office Q
(represented by ▦▦▦▦▦), served as a control, in that no special
effort was made to reduce costs during the past year.

RESULTS OF OFFICE COST REDUCTION PROGRAM

Expenses of Test and Control Groups for 1983
Expressed as Percentages of Same Expenses for 1982

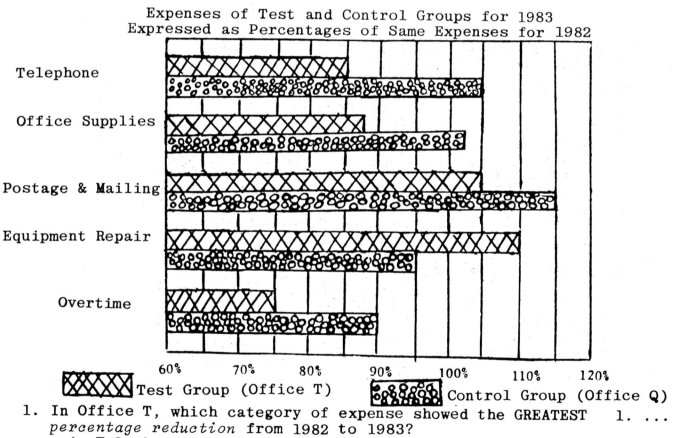

▨▨▨▨▨ Test Group (Office T)   ▦▦▦▦▦ Control Group (Office Q)

1. In Office T, which category of expense showed the GREATEST   1. ...
   percentage reduction from 1982 to 1983?
   A. Telephone   B. Office Supplies   C. Postage & Mailing
   D. Overtime
2. In which expense category did Office T show the BEST results   2. ...
   in *percentage terms*, when compared to Office Q?
   A. Telephone   B. Office Supplies   C. Postage & Mailing
   D. Overtime

5

3. According to the above chart, the cost reduction program was   3. ...
   LEAST effective for the expense category of
      A. Office Supplies   B. Postage & Mailing
      C. Equipment Repair   D. Overtime
4. Office T's telephone costs went down during 1983 by *approxi-*   4. ...
   mately how many percentage points?
      A. 15   B. 20   C. 85   D. 105
5. Which of the following changes occurred in expenses for Of-   5. ...
   fice Supplies in Office Q in the year 1983 as compared with
   the year 1982? They
      A. increased by more than 100% B. remained the same
      C. decreased by a few percentage points
      D. increased by a few percentage points
6. For which of the following expense categories do the results   6. ...
   in Office T and the results in Office Q differ *most nearly*
   by 10 percentage points?
      A. Telephone   B. Postage & Mailing
      C. Equipment Repair   D. Overtime
7. In which expense category did Office Q's costs show the   7. ...
   GREATEST *percentage increase* in 1983?
      A. Telephone   B. Office Supplies
      C. Postage & Mailing   D. Equipment Repair
8. In Office T, by *approximately* what percentage did overtime   8. ...
   expense CHANGE during the past year? It
      A. increased by 15%   B. increased by 75%
      C. decreased by 10%   D. decreased by 25%

TEST 5

Questions 1-5
DIRECTIONS: In answering questions 1 through 5, assume that you are in
charge of public information for an office which issues reports and
answers questions from other offices and from the public on changes in
land use. The charts below represent comparative land use in four neighborhoods. The area of each neighborhood is expressed in city blocks.
Assume that all city blocks are the same size.

NEIGHBORHOOD A - 16 CITY BLOCKS   **NEIGHBORHOOD B - 24 CITY BLOCKS**

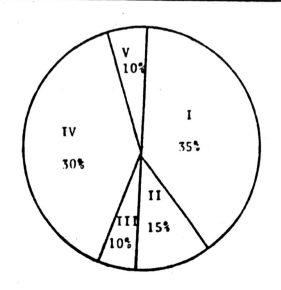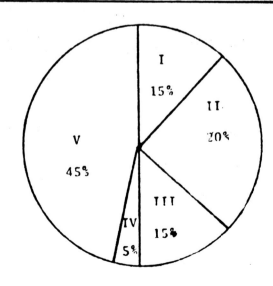

NEIGHBORHOOD C - 20 CITY BLOCKS   NEIGHBORHOOD D - 12 CITY BLOCKS

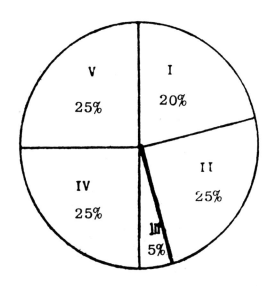
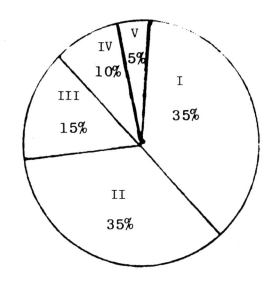

KEY

I - One-and two-family houses   III - Office buildings
II - Apartment buildings   IV - Retail stores
V - Factories and warehouses

1. In how many of these neighborhoods does residential use   1. ...
   (categories I and II together) account for *at least* 50% of
   the land use?
      A. One   B. Two   C. Three   D. Four
2. Which neighborhood has the LARGEST land area occupied by   2. ...
   apartment buildings? Neighborhood
      A. A   B. B   C. C   D. D
3. In which neighborhood is the LARGEST percentage of the   3. ...
   land devoted to *both* office buildings and retail stores?
   Neighborhood
      A. A   B. B   C. C   D. D
4. What is the DIFFERENCE, to the nearest city block, *between* 4. ...
   the amount of land devoted to retail stores in Neighborhood
   B and the amount devoted to similar use in Neighborhood C?
      A. 1 block   B. 2 blocks C. 4 blocks   D. 6 blocks
5. Which *one* of the following types of buildings occupies the 5. ...
   same amount of land area in Neighborhood B as the amount of
   land area occupied by retail stores in Neighborhood A?
      A. Factories and warehouses   B. Office buildings
      C. Retail stores   D. Apartment buildings

TEST 6

Questions 1-12.

ENROLLMENT IN POSTGRADUATE STUDIES

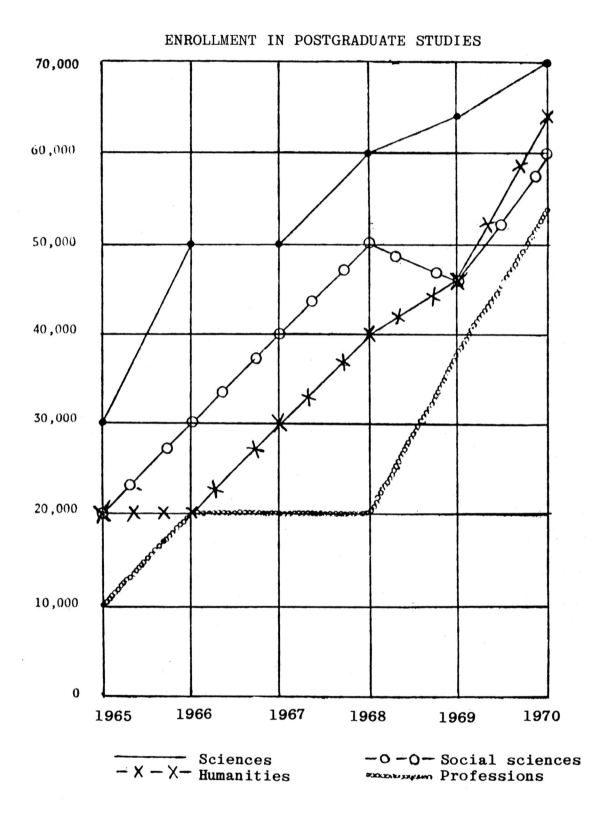

_____ Sciences   — O — O — Social sciences
— X — X — Humanities   xxxxxxxxx Professions

8

ENROLLMENT IN POSTGRADUATE STUDIES

Fields	Subdivisions	1969	1970
Sciences	Math	10,000	12,000
	Physical science	22,000	24,000
	Behavioral science	32,000	35,000
Humanities	Literature	26,000	34,000
	Philosophy	6,000	8,000
	Religion	4,000	6,000
	Arts	10,000	16,000
Social sciences	History	36,000	46,000
	Sociology	8,000	14,000
Professions	Law	2,000	2,000
	Medicine	6,000	8,000
	Business	30,000	44,000

1. The number of students enrolled in the social sciences and in 1. ....
   the humanities was the *same* in
   A. 1967 and 1960   B. 1965 and 1969
   C. 1969 and 1970   D. 1966 and 1969

2. A comparison of the enrollment of students in the various post-2. ....
   graduate studies shows that in every year from 1965 through
   1970 there were *more* students enrolled in the
   A. professions than in the sciences
   B. humanities than in the professions
   C. social sciences than in the professions
   D. humanities than in the sciences

3. The number of students enrolled in the humanities was greater 3. ....
   than the number of students enrolled in the professions by the
   same amount in
   A. two of the years   B. three of the years
   C. four of the years   D. five of the years

4. The *one* field of postgraduate study to show a DECREASE in en- 4. ....
   rollment in one year compared to the year immediately preceding
   is
   A. humanities B. sciences C. professions D. social sciences

5. If the proportion of arts students to all humanities students 5. ....
   was the same in 1967 as in 1970, then the number of arts students
   in 1967 was
   A. 7,500   B. 13,000   C. 15,000   D. 5,000

6. In which field of postgraduate study did enrollment INCREASE   6. ....
   BY 20 per cent from 1967 to 1968?
   A. Humanities B. Professions C. Sciences D. Social Sciences

7. The GREATEST increase in *overall* enrollment took place *between* 7. ....
   A. 1965 and 1966   B. 1967 and 1968
   C. 1968 and 1969   D. 1969 and 1970

8. Between 1967 and 1970, the *combined* enrollment of the sciences 8. ....
   and social sciences INCREASED BY
   A. 40,000   B. 48,000   C. 50,000   D. 54,000

9. If the enrollment in the social sciences had decreased from   9. ....
   1969 to 1970 at the same rate as from 1968 to 1969, then the
   social science enrollment in 1970 would have DIFFERED from the
   humanities enrollment in 1970,*most nearly*,by
   A. 6,000   B. 8,000   C. 12,000   D. 22,000

9

10. In the humanities, the GREATEST *percentage increase* in en-   10. ...
    rollment from 1969 to 1970 was in
    A. literature   B. philosophy   C. religion   D. arts
11. If the proportion of behavorial science students to the to-   11. ...
    tal number of students in the sciences was the *same* in 1966
    as in 1969, then the INCREASE in behavorial science enrollment
    from 1966 to 1970 was
    A. 5,000   B. 7,000   C. 10,000   D. 14,000
12. If enrollment in the professions increased at the *same* rate   12. ...
    from 1970 to 1971 as from 1969 to 1970, the enrollment in the
    professions in 1971 would be, *most nearly*,
    A. 85,000   B. 75,000   C. 60,000   D. 55,000

TEST 7

Questions 1-4.

BURGLARY RATE - METROPOLITAN CITY
1980-1985

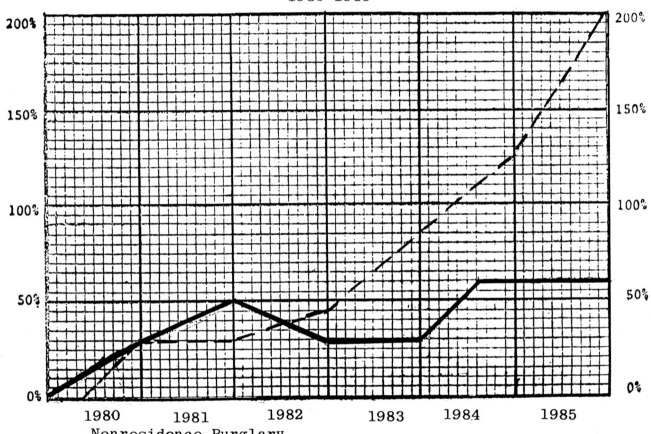

_____ Nonresidence Burglary
          Nighttime
- - - - Nonresidence Burglary
        Daytime
        1980-1985

1. At the beginning of *what* year was the percentage increase in   1. ...
   daytime and nighttime burglaries the SAME?
   A. 1981   B. 1982   C. 1983   D. 1985
2. In *what* year did the percentage of nighttime burglaries DE-   2. ...
   CREASE?
   A. 1980   B. 1982   C. 1983   D. 1985

3. In *what* year was there the MOST rapid increase in the percentage of daytime nonresidence burglaries?   3. ...
   A. 1981   B. 1983   C. 1984   D. 1985
4. At the end of 1984, the *actual* number of burglaries committed   4. ...
   in Metropolitan City
   A. was about 20%   B. was 40%   C. was 400
   D. cannot be determined from the information given

TEST 8

Questions 1-8.

TABLE A

PURCHASES MADE IN A MEAT MARKET
(Self-Service Refrigerated Meat Case)

Item	Printed Price Per Pound	Weight Indicated	Actual Weight	Price Per Package
Beef Liver	40¢	1 lb. 2 ozs.	1 lb. 2 ozs.	$ .50
Pork Loins:				
Rib End	29¢	2 lbs.4 ozs.	2 lbs.1 ozs.	.66
Loin End	32¢	1 lb. 8 ozs.	1 lb. 5 ozs.	.48
Veal Chops:				
Shoulder	70¢	2 lbs.8 ozs.	2 lbs. 2 ozs.	1.75
Rib	80¢	1 lb.10 ozs.	1 lb. 12 ozs.	1.50
Loin	90¢	3 lbs.2 ozs.	2 lbs.10 ozs.	2.85
Flank Steak	88¢	2 lbs.14ozs.	2 lbs. 3 ozs.	2.53
Cube Steak	80¢	12 ozs.	12 ozs.	.60
Top Sirloin Roast	99¢	1 lb.12 ozs.	1 lb. 8 ozs.	1.75
Fresh Ham	55¢	4 lbs.6 ozs.	4 lbs.	2.40
Bologna	40¢	6 ozs.	5 ozs.	.15
Frankfurters	45¢	1 lb. 4 ozs.	1 lb. 1 oz.	.57

TABLE B

PURCHASES MADE IN A CONFECTIONERY

Item	Price Quoted Per Pound	Amount Requested	Weights Used					Price Charged
			2 lb.	1 lb.	½ lb.	¼ lb.	1 oz.	
Chocolate Almonds	$1.12	3 1/4 lbs.	1	1	-	1	-	$3.64
Peanut Brittle	1.09	1 3/4 lbs.	-	1	1	1	-	1.91
Bridge Mix	1.25	5 ounces	-	-	-	1	1	.40
Special TV Mix	1.49	2 1/2 lbs.	1	-	1	-	-	3.75
Choc.Cherries	1.89	40 pieces	1	-	-	1	3	4.60
Caramels	1.05	4 lbs.	2	-	-	-	-	4.20
Cashew-Crunch	1.04	7 lbs.	2	2	1	2	-	7.28

11

Tables A and B represent hypothetical purchases made in a meat market and in a confectionery. In the case of the meat market, the price and weight figures were taken from the label on each meat package. The label gives the price per pound, the supposed weight of the package and the price of the package. In answering questions pertaining to the meat market, make no allowance for the weight of wrapping materials.

At the confectionery, all sales are weighed out on an even-balance scale using weights of various sizes. In checking the accuracy of the weights, it was found that the 1 oz. weights did actually weigh 1 oz. each, but that 1/4 lb. weights weighed 3 ozs. each, the 1/2 lb. weights weighed 6 ozs. each. the 1 lb. weights weighed 14 ozs. each and the 2 lb. weights weighed 1 lb. and 10 ozs. each. While the confectionery purchases were being made, note was taken of the weights used in weighing each purchase. The weights which were used are shown in Table B.

If you find, when computing the proper price of a meat or candy item, that the price comes out to a fractional part of a penny, assume that the proprietor is justified in charging a sum equal to the next higher penny. For example, if the computed price of an article is 38¼ cents, the proprietor may properly charge 39 cents.

1. If the weight indicated on the package containing veal chops(loin) 1. ..
   were accurate, the COST of the package should have been
   A. $2.36   B. $2.75   C. $2.79   D. $2.82
2. Based on the actual weight, *how much* should the package of bologna 2. ..
   have cost?
   A. 13¢   B. 14¢   C. 16¢   D. 17¢
3. The purchaser who bought the flank steak package OVERPAID, on the 3. ..
   basis of the actual weight of the package, by *approximately*
   A. 9¢   B. 53¢   C. 60¢   D. 69¢
4. The ACTUAL weight of *all* of the packages of meat shown in Table A 4. ..
   is
   A. 20 lbs. 8 ozs.   B. 20 lbs. 13 ozs.
   C. 23 lbs. 8 ozs.   D. none of the foregoing
5. *Each* chocolate cherry ACTUALLY weighs *approximately*   5. ..
   A. .2 oz.   B. .5 oz.   C. .8 oz.   D. 1.2 ozs.
6. The cashew-crunch purchase ACTUALLY weighed   6. ..
   A. 5 lbs. 9 ozs. B. 5 lbs. 12 ozs. C. 5 lbs. 15 ozs. D. 6 lbs. 2 ozs.
7. In accordance with the amount *actually* received, the chocolate al- 7. ..
   mond purchase SHOULD HAVE COST, *most nearly*,
   A. $2.31   B. $2.67   C. $2.80   D. $3.01
8. Which of the following *combinations* of weights used by the confec- 8. ..
   tionery would have come CLOSEST to giving the purchaser of the Special TV Mix the weight he requested?
   A. 1-2 lb. weight; 1-½ lb. weight B. 1-2 lb. weight; 2-½ lb. weights
   C. 1-2 lb. weight; 2-½ lb. weights; 1-1 oz. weight
   D. 1-2 lb. weight; 2-½ lb. weights; 2-1 oz. weights

KEYS (CORRECT ANSWERS)

TEST 1	TEST 2	TEST 3	TEST 4	TEST 5	TEST 6		TEST 7	TEST 8	
1. B	1. E	1. A	1. D	1. B	1. B	7. D	1. A	1. D	5. C
2. B	2. A	2. B	2. A	2. C	2. C	8. A	2. B	2. A	6. B
3. A	3. D	3. A	3. C	3. A	3. B	9. D	3. D	3. C	7. D
4. A			4. A	4. C	4. D	10. D	4. D	4. B	8. D
5. E			5. D	5. D	5. A	11. C			
			6. B		6. C	12. B			
			7. C						
			8. D						

FIRST AID

Table of Contents

Page

FIRST AID

Basic Principles and Practices

CAUTION
   These are emergency actions only. Always call a doctor if
possible. If you cannot get a doctor or trained first-aider
and the injured person is in danger of losing his life, take
one of the six emergency actions described in this section.

BUT, FIRST, OBSERVE THESE GENERAL RULES:
   Keep the injured person lying down, with his head level
with the rest of his body unless he has a head injury. In
that case raise his head slightly. Cover him and keep him
warm.
   Don't move the injured person to determine whether emergency
action is necessary. If he is NOT in danger of bleeding to
death, or is NOT suffocating or has NOT been severely burned,
or is NOT in shock, IT IS BETTER FOR THE UNTRAINED PERSON TO
LEAVE HIM ALONE.
   Do NOT give an unconscious or semiconscious person anything
to drink.
   Do NOT let an injured person see his wounds.
   Reassure him and keep him comfortable.

EMERGENCY ACTIONS
   I.   FOR BLEEDING
        TAKE THIS EMERGENCY ACTION
           Apply pressure directly over the wound. Use
        a first aid dressing, clean cloth, or even the
        bare hand. When bleeding has been controlled,
        add extra layers of cloth and bandage firmly.
        Do NOT remove the dressing. If the wound is in
        an arm or leg, elevate it with pillows or sub-
        stitutes. Do NOT use a tourniquet except as a
        last resort.

II. FOR BURNS

TAKE THIS EMERGENCY ACTION

Remove clothing covering the burn unless it sticks. Cover the burned area with a clean dry dressing or several layers of cloth folded into a pad. Apply a bandage over the pad, tightly enough to keep out the air. Don't remove the pad. DON'T USE GREASE, OIL OR ANY OINTMENT EXCEPT ON A DOCTOR'S ORDER. On chemical burns, such as caused by acid or lye, wash the burn thoroughly with water before covering with a dry dressing.

III. FOR BROKEN BONES

TAKE THIS EMERGENCY ACTION

Unless it is absolutely necessary to move a person with a broken bone, don't do anything except apply an ice bag to the injured area to relieve pain. If you must move him, splint the broken bone first so the broken bone ends cannot move. Use a board, thick bundle of newspapers, even a pillow. Tie the splint firmly in place above and below the break, but not tightly enough to cut off circulation. Use layers of cloth or newspapers to pad a hard splint.

Broken bones in the hand, arm, or shoulder should be supported by a sling after splinting. Use a triangular bandage or a substitute such as a scarf, towel, or torn width of sheet and tie the ends around the casualty's neck. Or place his forearm across his chest and pin his sleeve to his coat. In this way the lower sleeve will take the weight of the injured arm.

If you suspect a broken neck or back do not move the casualty except to remove him from further danger that may take his life. If you must remove the casualty, slide him gently onto a litter or a wide, rigid board. Then leave him alone until trained help arrives.

If a bone has punctured the skin, cover the wound with a first aid dressing or clean cloth and control bleeding by hand pressure.

IV. FOR SHOCK

TAKE THIS EMERGENCY ACTION

Shock may result from severe burns, broken bones, or other wounds, or from acute emotional disturbance. Usually the person going into shock becomes pale. His skin may be cold and moist. His pulse may be rapid. He may become wet with sweat. He may become unconscious.

Keep the casualty lying down. His head should be level with or lower than his body unless he has a head injury. In the latter case his head should be raised slightly. Wrap the casualty warm but do not permit him to become overheated. Try to avoid letting him see his injury. If he is able to swallow, give hime plenty of water to drink, with salt and baking soda added. Mix one teaspoonful of salt and one-half teaspoonful of baking soda to one quart of water. This will help to prevent severe shock.

Do NOT give anything by mouth to a person who is vomiting, is unconscious, or semiconscious, or has an abdominal wound.

V. FOR SUFFOCATION

TAKE THIS EMERGENCY ACTION

Suffocation can result from pressure on the neck or chest, contact with a live electric wire, drowning or breathing-in foreign substances such as liquids, smoke, or gas. The usual signs of suffocation are coughing and sputtering or other difficulty in breathing. As breathing becomes difficult or stops, the face may turn purple and lips and fingernails become blue. Unconsciousness will follow quickly unless you act at once.

First, remove the person from the cause of suffocation. If he is in contact with a live wire, don't touch him. Shut off the current if you can. If not, stand on a piece of dry wood or on paper and remove the wire from the person with a long dry stick or other nonmetallic object.

If the person is in a room filled with gas, smoke, or water, get him out quickly. Remove any objects from his mouth or throat that may obstruct breathing. Then apply artificial respiration immediately, as follows:

ARTIFICIAL RESPIRATION

Mouth-to-Mouth (Mouth-to-Nose) Method

Tilt the head back so the chin is pointing upward, and pull or push the jaw into a jutting out position. (These maneuvers should relieve obstruction of the airway by moving the base of the tongue away from the back of the throat.)

Open your mouth wide and place it tightly
over the casualty's nostrils shut or close
the nostrils with your cheek. Or close the
casualty's mouth and place your mouth over
the nose. Blow into his mouth or nose.
(Air may be blown through the casualty's
teeth, even though they may be clenched.)
The first blowing efforts should determine
whether or not obstruction exists.

Remove your mouth, turn your head to the
side, and listen for the return rush of air
that indicates air-exchange. Repeat the
blowing effort. For an adult, blow vigor-
ously at the rate of 12 breaths per minute.
For a child, take relatively shallow breaths
appropriate for the child's size at the rate
of about 20 per minute.

If you are not getting air-exchange, recheck
the head and jaw position. If you still do
not get air-exchange, quickly turn the casualty
on his side and administer several sharp blows
between the shoulder blades in the hope of
dislodging foreign matter. Again sweep your
fingers through the casualty's mouth to remove
any foreign matter.

Those who do not wish to come in contact with
the person may hold a cloth over the casualty's
mouth or nose and breathe through it. The
cloth does not greatly affect the exchange of air.

Mouth-To-Mouth Technique For Infants And Small
Children

If foreign matter is visible in the mouth, wipe
it out quickly with your fingers or a cloth wrapped
around your fingers.

Place the child on his back and use the fingers
of both hands to lift the lower jaw from beneath
and behind, so that it juts out.

Place your mouth over the child's mouth and nose
making a relatively leakproof seal, and breathe
into the child, using shallow puffs of air. The
breathing rate should be about 20 per minute.

If you meet resistance in your blowing efforts,
recheck the position of the jaw. If the air
passages are still blocked, the child should be
suspended momentarily by the ankles or inverted
over one arm and given two or three sharp pats
between the shoulder blades, in the hope of dislodging obstructing matter.

Other Manual Methods Of Artificial Respiration

Persons who cannot, or will not, use the mouth-to-mouth (mouth-to-nose) method of artificial respiration should use another manual method. The nature of the injury in any given case may prevent the use of one method, while favoring another. Other methods suggested for use by the American National Red Cross are THE CHEST PRESSURE-ARM LIFT METHOD (Silvester) and THE BACK PRESSURE-ARM LIFT METHOD (Holger-Nielsen).

When performing any method of artificial respiration, remember to time your efforts to coincide with the casualty's first attempt to breathe for himself.

Be sure that the air passages are clear of all obstructions, that the casualty is positioned in a manner that will keep the air passages clear, and that air is forced into the lungs as soon as possible.

If vomiting occurs, quickly turn the casualty on his side, wipe out his mouth, and reposition him.

When the casualty is revived, keep him as quiet as possible until he is breathing regularly. Loosen his clothing, cover him to keep him warm, and then treat for shock.

Whatever method of artificial respiration you use, it should be continued until the casualty begins to breathe for himself, or until there is no doubt that the person is dead.

VI.   TO MOVE INJURED PERSONS
        TAKE THIS EMERGENCY ACTION
        Do NOT move an injured person except to prevent further injury or possible death. If you must move him, keep him lying down flat. Move him on a wide board, such as an ironing board or door, and tie him to it so he won't roll off.

If you have nothing to carry him on, get two other persons to help you carry. You must kneel together on the same side of the casualty and slide your hands under him gently. Then lift carefully, keeping his body level. Walk in step to prevent jarring, and carry him only far enough to remove from danger.

———

CURRENT CHANGES IN FIRST-AID METHODS

When an accident occurs and before medical help arrives, the victim often can be helped by someone who has knowledge of first aid. However, a person who does not know the recent developments in treatment may find that he is endangering the physical well being of the victim by using an improper method. Many of the methods once used are now obsolete. For example:

CUTS

   OLD METHOD
   Apply an antiseptic such as iodine, to a cut to kill germs.

   CURRENT METHOD
   Wash the cut with gauze dipped in soap and water. Antiseptics can destroy living tissue around the wound and retard healing. Soap and water, however does not destroy tissue, and it provides a flushing action that washes away dirt and some bacteria.

BLEEDING FROM ARTERY

   OLD METHOD
   Apply a tourniquet to stop bleeding from a cut artery.

   CURRENT METHOD
   The best way to control any bleeding is to apply sterile compresses directly over the wound, and bandage them tightly in place. The pressure of the bandage will stem the flow of blood. Medical attention is indicated for any cut artery. The old method of using a tourniquet, say medical authorities, can be dangerous because it cuts off all circulation to the limb, which can lead to a risk of gangrene and even amputation. Also, if muscles begin to die from lack of oxygen, poisonous substances may form and get into the victim's circulation, causing "tourniquet shock."

CHOKING

   CURRENT METHOD
   Perform the Heimlich method by hugging the victim with his back against your body, placing your arms around his body. Make a fist with one hand, hold your fist with the other hand and place it under victim's diaphragm and forcefully push air up forcing food up windpipe and out of mouth. If necessary, make several separate forceful movements until successful.

OLD METHOD
    If a person is choking, slap him on the back repeatedly
in order to dislodge the obstruction.
    Do nothing for a while in order to give the per-
son's voice box (where food usually lodges) enough
time to relax. At this stage the person ordinarily
coughs up the object. If nothing happens and the
person stops breathing, lean him forward, then slap
him on the back to dislodge the obstruction. A
young child may be held upside down to help dislodge
any obstruction. If the obstruction can be reached
with the fingers, it should be removed. Slapping a
person immediately may cause the object to be sucked,
by a sudden rush of air, into his windpipe. If the
object has slipped into the windpipe, a slap may make
him cough, forcing the object up against the narrower
opening of the vocal cords. This can cause a blockage
and asphyxiation.

BURNS

OLD METHOD
    When someone is burned, apply butter or other house-
hold grease to the area.

CURRENT METHOD
    Never apply grease. The sterility of household
greases cannot be guaranteed and therefore there is
a risk of introducing infection. In serious burns,
any grease or ointment must be scraped off before
treatment at a hospital, and the patient experiences
more pain. If the burn is minor (one that does not
require medical attention and when the skin is not
broken), sterile commercial products can be used.
Another method is to submerge the burned area in cold
water (under 70 degrees) and keep adding ice to maintain the temperature. Parts that cannot be submerged
should be treated with a cloth dipped in cold water.
Treatment should continue until the burned parts can
be kept out of the cold water without recurrence of
pain. However, there is still some controversy about
the use of this treatment when the burn is extensive.
In a serious burn, the Red Cross recommends the application of a dry sterile dressing, bandaged securely
in place to protect the burn from contamination and to
prevent exposure to air.

DIVING ACCIDENT

OLD METHOD
    If a person diving into the water appears to have
struck his head, pull him out of the water as quickly
as possible.

CURRENT METHOD

Many cases of paralysis have resulted from rough handling of a person dragged out of the water. Instead, the person should be supported in the water and kept afloat until the ambulance arrives. Quite often in this type of accident, the person's neck is fractured, and moving his head roughly is likely to cause irreparable injury to the spinal cord. If, however, it is necessary to remove a person from the water, he should be placed on something rigid so that his head will be at the same level as his body.

NOSEBLEED

OLD METHOD

Use an ice pack to stop a nosebleed.

CURRENT METHOD

Tilt the person's head all the way back so that his nose becomes the highest point of his body, and pinch his nostrils. It is important to keep the head tilted to lessen pressure. However, if the bleeding is severe, roll a piece of gauze and use it to plug his nostril, making sure that a long piece hangs out to facilitate removal. Gentle pressure can be exerted on the outside of the nostril. In severe bleeding, it is necessary to have medical attention.

POISON

OLD METHOD

Use a mixture of burned toast, tea and milk to counteract accidental swallowing of poisons.

CURRENT METHOD

Poison-control authorities say that the homemade antidote of burned toast, tea and milk is useless because the charcoal from the toast is not the kind that absorbs poisons. Call a physician immediately. Begin mouth-to-mouth resuscitation if the victim has difficulty breathing. Actually, the nature of the poison will determine the first-aid measure to use. Give water or milk. Do NOT induce vomiting if a petroleum product, such as gasoline, kerosene or turpentine has been ingested. With poisons such as an overdose of aspirin, induce vomiting by either placing a finger at the back of the victim's throat, or by giving salt water (two teaspoons to a glass) or syrup of ipecac (one ounce for adults and half an ounce for children).

ACCIDENT

OLD METHOD
Rush a person to the hospital as quickly as possible after an accident.

CURRENT METHOD
Proper carrying of an injured person is necessary in order to avoid the possibility of permanent damage. To move a person too quickly may cause spinal injury, hemorrhage or shock. Unless the person must be moved out of danger, it is BEST to apply first aid on the spot and wait until the ambulance arrives. The American Red Cross says: "The principle of first aid is to get the victim to medical attention in the best possible manner."

FIRST AID SUMMARY CHART

FOR THESE PURPOSES	USE THESE	OR THESE	SUGGESTED QUANTITY
For open wounds, scratches, and cuts. Not for burns.	1. Antiseptic Solution: Benzalkonium Chloride Solution, U.S.P., 1 to 1,000 parts of water.	Quaternary ammonium compounds in water. Sold under trade names as Zephiran, Phemerol, Ceepryn, and Bactine.	3-to 6-oz. bottle.
For faintness, adult dose 1/2 teaspoon in cup of water; children 5 to 10 drops in 1/2 glass of water. As smelling salts, remove stopper, hold bottle under nose.	2. Aromatic Spirits of ammonia.		1-to 2-oz. bottle.
For shock -- dissolve 1 teaspoonful salt and 1/2 teaspoonful baking soda in 1 quart water. Have patient drink as much as he will. Don't give to unconscious person or semiconscious person. If using substitutes dissolve six 10-gr. sodium chloride tablets and six 5-gr. sodium bicarbonate (or sodium citrate) tablets in 1 qt. water.	3. Table salt.	Sodium chloride tablets, 10 gr., 50 tablets in bottle.	1 box.
	4. Baking soda.	Sodium bicarbonate or sodium citrate tablets, 5 gr., 50 tablets in bottle.	8-to 10 oz. box.
For a sling; as a cover; for a dressing.	5. Triangular bandage, folded, 37 by 37 by 52 in., with 2 safety pins.	Muslin or other strong material. Cut to exact dimensions. Fold and wrap each bandage and 2 safety pins separately in paper.	4 bandages.

FIRST AID SUMMARY CHART (Cont'd)

THESE PURPOSES	USE THESE	OR THESE	SUGGESTED QUANTITY
open wounds or dry dressings burns. These packaged rile.	6. Two medium first aid dressings, folded, sterile with gauze enclosed cotton pads, 8 in. by 7 1/2 in. Packaged with muslin bandage and 4 safety pins.	a) Two emergency dressings 8 in. by 7 1/2 in., in glassine bags, sterilized. One roller bandage, 2 in. by 10 yds. b) Four large sanitary napkins wrapped separately and sterilized. One roller bandage, 2 in. by 10 yards.	As indicated.
open wounds or dry dressings burns. These packaged rile.	7. Two small first aid dressings, folded, sterile with gauze enclosed cotton pads and gauze bandage, 4 in. by 7 in.	Twelve sterile gauze pads in individual packages, 3 in. by 3 in. One roller bandage, 1 in. by 10 yards.	As indicated.
eyes irritated dust, smoke, or es. Use 2 drops each eye. Apply d compresses ry 20 minutes possible.	8. Eye drops.	Bland eye sold by druggists under various trade names.	1/2-to 1-oz. bottle with dropper.
splinting broken gers or other ll bones and for rring solutions.	9. Twelve tongue blades, wooden.	Shingles, pieces of orange crate, or other light wood cut to approximately 1 1/2 in. by 6 in.	As indicated.

FIRST AID SUMMARY CHART (Cont'd)

FOR THESE PURPOSES	USE THESE	OR THESE	SUGGESTED QUANTITY
or purifying water hen it cannot be oiled. (Radio- ctive contamination annot be neutralized r removed by boiling r by disinfectants.)	10.Water purifi- cation tablets Iodine (trade names--Globa line, Bursoline, Potable Aqua) Chlorine (trade name--Halazone).	Tincture of iodine or iodine solution (3 drops per quart of water). Household bleach (approx. 5% available chlorine) 3 drops per quart of water.	Tablets-- Bottle of 50 or 100. Liquid-- One Small bottle.
or bandages or dress- ngs: Old soft towels nd sheets are best. ut in sizes necessary o cover wounds. Tow- ls are burn dressings. lace over burns and asten with triangular andage or strips of heet. Towels and heets should be laun- ered, ironed and pack- ged in heavy paper. elaunder every 3 months.	11.Large bath towels.		2.
	12.Small bath towels.		2.
	13.Bed Sheet.		1.
or administering stimu- ants and liquids.	14.Paper drinking cups.		25 to 50.
lectric lights may go ut. Wrap batteries eparately in moisture- roof covering. Don't eep in flashlight.	15.Flashlight.		1.
	16.Flashlight batteries.		3.
or holding bandages in lace.	17.Safety pins, 1 1/2 in. long.		12 to 15.
or cutting bandages nd dressings, or for emoving clothing from njured body surface.	18.Razor blades, single edge.	Sharp knife or scissors.	3.
or cleansing skin.	19.Toilet soap	Any mild soap.	1 bar.
or measuring or tirring solutions.	20.Measuring spoons.	Inexpensive plas- tic or metal.	1 set.
or splinting broken rms or legs.	21.Twelve splints, plastic or wooden, 1/8 to 1 1/4 in. thick, 3 1/2 in. wide by 12 to 15 in. long.	A 40-page news- paper folded to dimensions, pieces of orange crate sidings, or shingles cut to size.	As indicated

ANSWER SHEET

TEST NO. _____ PART _____ TITLE OF POSITION _____

(AS GIVEN IN EXAMINATION ANNOUNCEMENT - INCLUDE OPTION, IF ANY)

PLACE OF EXAMINATION _____ DATE _____

(CITY OR TOWN)   (STATE)

RATING

USE THE SPECIAL PENCIL.   MAKE GLOSSY BLACK MARKS.

Make only ONE mark for each answer.   Additional and stray marks may be counted as mistakes.   In making corrections, erase errors COMPLETELY.

ANSWER SHEET

USE THE SPECIAL PENCIL.   MAKE GLOSSY BLACK MARKS.

	A B C D E		A B C D E		A B C D E		A B C D E		A B C D E
1		26		51		76		101	
2		27		52		77		102	
3		28		53		78		103	
4		29		54		79		104	
5		30		55		80		105	
6		31		56		81		106	
7		32		57		82		107	
8		33		58		83		108	
9		34		59		84		109	
10		35		60		85		110	

Make only ONE mark for each answer.   Additional and stray marks may be
counted as mistakes.   In making corrections, erase errors COMPLETELY.

	A B C D E		A B C D E		A B C D E		A B C D E		A B C D E
11		36		61		86		111	
12		37		62		87		112	
13		38		63		88		113	
14		39		64		89		114	
15		40		65		90		115	
16		41		66		91		116	
17		42		67		92		117	
18		43		68		93		118	
19		44		69		94		119	
20		45		70		95		120	
21		46		71		96		121	
22		47		72		97		122	
23		48		73		98		123	
24		49		74		99		124	
25		50		75		100		125	